To:
Bethany;
May God Bless
and Keep you always.

Gwen Mosley

TRUSTING
GOD
Daily

A HEAVENLY DEVOTIONAL

Gwendolyn F. Mosley

WESTBOW
PRESS®
A DIVISION OF THOMAS NELSON
& ZONDERVAN

WestBow Press books may be ordered through booksellers or by contacting:

WestBow Press
A Division of Thomas Nelson & Zondervan
1663 Liberty Drive
Bloomington, IN 47403
www.westbowpress.com
1 (866) 928-1240

Scripture taken from the Amplified Bible, Copyright © 1954, 1958, 1962, 1964, 1965, 1987 by The Lockman Foundation. Used by permission.

ISBN: 978-1-9736-8136-6 (sc)
ISBN: 978-1-9736-8135-9 (e)

Print information available on the last page.

WestBow Press rev. date: 09/02/2020

This devotional is dedicated to my husband, Stan, the love of my life

Also, my 3 sons Kevin, Donavan, and Kenneth

They have each encouraged and inspired
me to complete this work of love

God has poured these words into my spirit to put on each page. What a blessing to be used to bless the lives of others. These devotionals are a testament to my relationship with a loving God, merciful Jesus, and dynamic Holy Spirit. It took many years, but it has been well worth every minute. God has entrusted me with these nuggets to be shared with others. I will be forever grateful!

Foreword

The Believer's walk with God is not deemed meaningful based solely upon years of knowledge about God. Longevity is not key. I believe the most important aspect of our relationship with the Father of the universe is NOW. This moment. And then the next. Day by day, we experience meaningful moments with God, and as we navigate life's ever-changing roads, we realize with more clarity that His promise to never leave nor forsake us is solid and supreme. But we don't reach tomorrow having skipped today.

This book, Trusting God Daily, helps us to put life's challenges into proper perspective each day as we address everyday obstacles through the eyes of faith. We can be assured that even though this world brings times of trouble, we have a hope and an anchor in Jesus, who has already overcome the world.

I have watched this excellent teacher, my mother, live these principles from her heart, not just her lips — often not with her spoken words at all. Her life of faith has been an inspiration to me, but has also been instilled in me. From her years of diligent counsel and instruction from God's Word to a daily example of wholeheartedly following a life of love and faith, even in dark times, I can tell you this. Gwendolyn F. Mosley isn't just writing a book here. This is a memoir and testament of an intimate and deep-grounding of mustard seed faith that has sprung up to become a flourishing tree of life.

Enjoy!

-Kenneth Mosley

Introduction

There's one thing I've learned in this life here on earth. I have to trust God daily with my life. To acquire success, it is absolutely necessary to check things out with Him. We have an eternal GPS system installed in us by our divine Master, God. This system gives us the directions in detail that we need to make it through the obstacles of life. As the driver of our vehicle, we control the way we want to go through life. So, ultimately it is up to us to choose to use what God has already put in place for us to achieve success. I marvel at the way the modern technology of our cell phones can give us the location and direction of our destination anywhere we find ourselves. It could be a local or distant direction we need, yet, the satellite can tell us whether to go north, south, east, or west. It can tell us if we should turn right or left (that's my kind of directions). So, no matter where we are, we can find our way to our desired location.

Well, God has placed this eternal system inside of us as an internal compass. All we have to do is check it out every time we feel we are losing our way. He gave us an external map, the Bible, to guide us along our journey through life. Whenever I took road trips with my mom, she would pull out her trusty map and highlight the pathway she wanted to take. It told us the streets and highways we needed to take to reach our destination. I was the driver and she was the navigator. She would tell me what the map said for us to do and I would follow her directions. Likewise, our heavenly Father has the eternal plan for each of our lives. Jesus has prepared the way for us to go, and the Holy Spirit is the navigator of the journey. Although my mom was the navigator, as the driver, I had the right to choose whether or not I was going to listen to what she was saying as we traveled along the journey. Since she was looking at the map, the wise thing for me to do was to follow her directions. Once in a while, I would try following my own bright idea and we would wind up lost. Then, she would refer to the map and get us back on track.

Life is much like that. As long as we choose to follow the map designed by the divine engineer, stay on the designated route already prepared for us, and listen to the navigator, we will get to our desired destination with very few detours. The more detours we encounter, the longer it will take for us to achieve our expected end. Through trial and error, I have found out that going off with my own plan has cost me wasted time and effort. Following the plan already designed for my journey and success saves precious time and effort. Reading these devotionals will assist you in reaching your destination in life. Please choose to listen to the navigator as your guide for a successful journey on a daily basis. These portions of the Word of God will encourage you to stay on course. Hopefully, these daily thoughts will inspire you to press on as you travel down the road of life. The declarations and confessions will help you to stand on the Word you just read. Finally, the prayers and reflections are acknowledgements of our need to submit to the awesome plan of victory for our lives!

Contents

Memory Verse: Hebrews 10:35, 36 Cast not away therefore your confidence, which hath great recompense of reward. For ye have need of patience, that, after ye have done the will of God, ye might receive the promise.

Thought For The Day: "Lord, Am I Doing Your Will?"

Sometimes it's hard to tell if we are in the "perfect will of God" for our lives. We get a message from Him and begin to pursue the directive we've been given. The excitement we feel inside gives us the zeal to persevere against the obstacles that try to get in our way. We are confident in what God has said, what we are to do, and what we will receive. As time goes by, that zeal and confidence begins to dwindle under the reality of life's situations and circumstances. We know in our spirit that we are an overcomer and not a succumber, but we just can't tell anymore if we are pursuing God's will for our life.

If you have felt the sting of doubt, you know how it feels to be in this predicament. This scripture tells us not to fling away our fearless confidence, for it carries a great and glorious compensation of reward. The problem we face is having the patience and endurance it takes to perform and fully accomplish the will of God for our life. Doing this will cause us to receive and enjoy the promise of God. Because the Spirit of God, in us, contains the fruit of patience and endurance; we have what it takes to win. The struggle is to keep our eyes on the prize of the high calling of Christ Jesus and not on the storms of life. If we can stay focused on what God has said and promised, we can obtain the prize. Our relationship with He, who is more than enough, can prevail as we live by faith in Him. So, let's be strong, bold, and of good courage; knowing that God will perform His perfect Will for our lives, if we let Him.

Declaration and Confession:

God has not given me the spirit of fear, but of love, power, and a sound mind. I have the mind of Christ. I think like Him and act like Him. I will not allow the storms of life to detour my journey. I speak to the winds and the waves and I say, "peace be still, in the name of Jesus." I will not fling away my confidence in the Almighty God of Promise. I am the just and I live by faith. When activated, my faith overcomes the fear or false evidence appearing real the enemy brings. I am bold, strong, and encouraged by the greater One that's in me! I will receive my just reward!

Prayer:

Dear Lord Jesus,

Help me to be single-minded in my pursuit of the promises you have made to me. I have the mind of Christ. I walk by faith and not by sight. I will follow the directions you have given me, without fear. Thank you for allowing me the privilege to do your will in the earth. Use me to be the bold soldier you have called me to be. I have on your armor, because I am in a battle. I will activate it, so I can win! I am fully persuaded and confident in who I am in Christ Jesus and will obtain the prize. In Jesus' mighty name, Amen.

Reflections:

In what areas of your life do you need to surrender your will to God's purpose for you?

Gwendolyn F. Mosley

Memory Verse: Romans 12:1, 2 I appeal to you therefore, brethren, and beg of you in view of [all] the mercies of God, to make a decisive dedication of your bodies [presenting all your members and faculties] as a living sacrifice, holy (devoted, consecrated) and well pleasing to God, which is your reasonable (rational, intelligent) service and spiritual worship. Do not be conformed to this world (this age), [fashioned after and adapted to its external, superficial customs], but be transformed (changed) by the [entire] renewal of your mind [by its new ideals and its new attitude], so that you may prove [for yourselves] what is the good and acceptable and perfect will of God even the thing which is good and acceptable and perfect [in His sight for you].

Thought for the Day: "Captive Thoughts"

*B*ecause we are housed in these bodies of clay, it is easy to allow ourselves to be subject to the thoughts of the flesh. As we consider the Words of our heavenly Father, we realize that our daily thoughts don't compare to His. It is important that we delete these earthly thoughts from the memory bank of our mind. God has equipped us with an arsenal that will take hold of these thoughts and dethrone them in our lives. Any argument, theory, reasoning, or proud thing that claims to be higher than God in our lives must be dealt with.

When we renew our minds with the Word of God, we are gathering the weapons that will bring victory into our lives. God's Word opposes the words of this world. As a result, we find ourselves in the middle of a conflict. Our minds are the battleground for this warfare. There is a "tug of war" going on in our minds. Every time we allow the Word of God to override the words of the world, we take that thought captive and it is deleted from our mind. Eventually, we will have more of the Word of God in our memory bank than the words of this world. When this happens, God's thoughts will reign supreme in our minds and we will be set free from the thoughts of the flesh.

Declaration and Confession:

God has equipped me with the mighty weapons of His Word. Although I live in this body of flesh, I will not allow it's thoughts to rule in my life. I will take my daily training in His Word and exercise it in my thoughts. The words of this world will become captive to the Words of God in my life. I will obey God's Word and dethrone the words of this world. I am victorious, because I know God, Jesus is my Messiah, and I am empowered by the Holy Spirit!

Prayer:

Dear Heavenly Father,

I am thankful to you for giving me the victory over the things of this world. Your thoughts are higher than my thoughts. I acknowledge who you are in my life today. Your Word is truth. I hide your Word in my heart today, so I won't sin against you. Every thought that does not acknowledge who you are and tries to exalt itself above you, I take captive right now. You are well able to do all things in my life. There is absolutely nothing that is too hard for you to do. I submit my will, my emotions, and every thought to my knowledge of who you are. You are a great and mighty God! I cast everything upon you that would try to convince me that I am defeated. Thank you for the victory in my life today! In the mighty name of Jesus, Amen.

Reflections:

What scripture(s) would help you overcome persisting negative thought patterns?

Memory Verse: Psalms 139:13 – 17 For You did form my inward parts; You did knit me together in my mother's womb. I will confess and praise You for You are fearful and wonderful and for the awful wonder of my birth! Wonderful are Your works, and that my inner self knows right well. My frame was not hidden from You when I was being formed in secret [and] intricately and curiously wrought [as if embroidered with various colors] in the depths of the earth [a region of darkness and mystery]. Your eyes saw my unformed substance, and in Your book all the days [of my life] were written before ever they took shape, when as yet there was none of them. How precious and weighty also are Your thoughts of me, O God! How vast is the sum of them!

Thought for the Day: Fearfully and Wonderfully Made!

The controversy continues in regard to abortion. This is a very sticky subject and is about to go to vote in our area. Women are fighting for the right to abort the baby (fetus) in their womb depending on the circumstances that surround the conception process. Is it the right of the woman to choose what should be done to her body or the right of a child to be born? Who is responsible for life to begin with? How did the woman obtain her body? Should it be called murder before or after the birth of a child? Whose freedoms are really being violated? How will these actions be judged? Who will be judged for these actions? Who has the right to judge? These are just some of the questions that we need to think about. However, this particular scripture tells us that God is responsible for forming us in our mother's womb. We are not an accident, because God has given great thought about who we are and what we are to accomplish while we are in the earth. His desire for our destiny has already been set by Him, before we are born. We can only praise and worship Him for the miraculous event of birth!

Although the workings of our very being are intricate, causing us to be fearfully and wonderfully made, how we feel about who we are can make a huge difference in what happens during our life. God has a wonderful plan for each of us, but our right to choose can make or break His plan. The choices of those who conceive us play a monumental part in our beginning advantage or disadvantage in life. Yet, I'm so glad that Our God is Awesome and can turn evil to good, if we let Him. The right to choose is ordained by God. Hopefully, we consider what lines up with His plan and what doesn't, before we choose. However, He has taken our human frailties into consideration. So, He gives us chances to repent and start over. Because of His sacrifice of Jesus, there is a way out of our troubles. Hopefully, we won't allow the opinions of others to cause us to belittle who we really are. We must look at ourselves through the eyes of the creator of life to get an accurate read on who we are. We need to think about ourselves like He thinks, because what we think in our heart determines who we believe we are. I want God to search my heart, so my thoughts will line up with His. Then, I can say with confidence, "I am fearfully and wonderfully made!"

Declaration and Confession:

I am fearfully and wonderfully made! God has a good plan for my life. I will listen to what He has to say about who I am. His thoughts of good for my life are too numerous to count! I will not listen to anyone else. My own thoughts must line up with His. I want to carry out His plan for my life! I am who God says I am!

Prayer:

Dear Father God,

Thank you for the privilege of being born into the earth! I did not bring myself here. You ordained that I be born. No matter what happened during my conception, I give you permission to take over my life. Help me to see myself the way you do. I want the thoughts in my heart to line up with yours. I believe I am fearfully and wonderfully made! In Jesus' Mighty Name, Amen.

Reflection:

Make a list. What are five God-given qualities that you possess that are unique and wonderful?

Memory Verse: 1 Samuel 17:45, 46, 50, 50, 51 Then said David to the Philistine, You come to me with a sword, a spear, and a javelin, but I come to you in the name of the Lord of hosts, the God of the ranks of Israel. Whom you have defied. This day the Lord will deliver you into my hand, and I will smite you and cut off your head. And I will give the corpses of the army of the Philistines this day to the birds of the air and the wild beasts of the earth, that all the earth may know that there is a God in Israel. So, David prevailed over the Philistine with a sling and with a stone, and struck down the Philistine and slew him. But no sword was in David's hand. So he ran and stood over the Philistine, took his sword and drew it out of its sheath, and killed him, and cut off his head with it. When the Philistines saw that their mighty champion was dead, they fled.

Thought for the Day: That Giant Will Die!

Like most children, I loved hearing the story of David and Goliath. It's much better than the stories of today about the super heroes. Goliath is described as a champion of the Philistines who was 10 feet tall. He wore a bronze helmet and a coat of bronze that weighed approximately 156 pounds. He had on bronze shin armor and a bronze javelin across his shoulders. The head of his spear weighed 19 pounds. He stood and shouted insults to the ranks of Israel for 40 days. Then came David, the little shepherd boy who had killed the lion and the bear to protect his father's sheep. He was symbolic of the Good Shepherd [Jesus] who refused to allow the enemy to harm His sheep. He was sent to the battlefield by his father, Jesse. Yet, when he got there, he was ridiculed for coming by his oldest brother Eliab. He told him to go back and tend his few sheep. He got mad at David, because he asked the men a good question. What will the man who kills this Philistine get for a reward? David couldn't understand how these mighty men of valor who served in the armies of the living God could be such cowards! How would you like your little brother to come in the midst of your squadron and call you and your buddies cowards? David ignored his brother and kept inquiring about the reward. Whoever killed the Philistine would receive great riches from the king, as well as, his daughter. Also, his father's house would be free from taxes and service in Israel. Saul called for David and he told the king he would take care of the Philistine. Saul told him he was an adolescent and that Goliath had been a warrior from his youth. So, David explained to him that he too was a warrior tending his father's sheep. Well, you know what happened. Saul tried to dress him in his armor, but that didn't work. Instead, David challenged Goliath, who thought he was a big joke and killed him with a smooth stone and a sling!

We all face giants in our life at one time or the other. Just as Jesus endured 40 days and nights, while fasting in the wilderness, we can expect no less. We will have times of testing and trials. David represented judgment against the enemy who defied the ranks of Israel for those 40 days. At the end of Jesus' test in the wilderness, He defeated the enemy who challenged His position in the Kingdom of God! He brought judgment by using the Word of God! These are two excellent examples of how God wants us to respond to the insults of the enemy that come our way. The giants that come our way may be in the form of sickness and disease; financial woes or mental and emotional attacks. However they present themselves, we belong to a God who can deliver us out of the hands of the enemy. All we have to do is believe His Word over the words of the enemy and we can't be sidetracked by the nay Sayers. We have to stand our ground and fight the good fight of faith! Then, that giant that's taunting us will die!

Declaration and Confession:

I belong to the King of Kings and Lord of Lords! I represent the Kingdom of God in the earth. I have the Victory over every challenge that comes my way, because Jesus has already made me Victorious. He said He would never leave me or forsake me. The Greater One lives on the inside of me! The God who has delivered me before will deliver me now! The giants in my life must die!

Prayer:

Dear Lord Jesus,

Thank you for giving me the Victory over every obstacle in my life that tries to keep me from the promises of God. Every battle I face is Yours and You will defeat my enemies! In Jesus' Mighty Name, Amen.

Reflection:

Remember your former giants; what has God caused you to overcome already? And what are you trusting Him for victory today?

Memory Verse: Philippians 2:8 – 11 And after he had appeared in human form, He abased and humbled Himself [still further] and carried His obedience to the extreme of death, even the death of the cross! Therefore [because He stooped so low] God has highly exalted Him and has freely bestowed on Him the name that is above every name. That in (at) the name of Jesus every knee should (must) bow, in heaven and on earth and under the earth. And every tongue [frankly and openly] confess and acknowledge that Jesus Christ is Lord, to the glory of God the Father.

Thought for the Day: "Your Knee Will Bow!"

---

*T*he form of government in a country ruled by a king or queen is called a monarchy. The king and queen along with their descendants are considered to be royalty. They have the highest rank or title in their country. The people of that country are called subjects, because they are subject to the authority of the king or queen. They would not dare go before the king or queen without acknowledging their authority and power. So, those who are not nobility may bow in reverence to the king or queen, when they are in their presence. The region or country where they rule is called a kingdom.

Jesus left His heavenly kingdom to walk the earth, as a man, in order to redeem us to His Father. He became a sacrifice to rescue us from the clutches of sin and death. The only way He could do that was to die on the cross and present His blood to His Father. Doing this set us free by giving us the right to choose Him as Savior and Lord. If we choose to accept Him as the sacrifice that He became for us, we become part of the Kingdom of God. We are subject to the authority of the King! Unlike an earthly king, God the Father, Jesus His son, and the Holy Spirit will not force us to submit to their authority. It is merely an act of our will. If we choose to be part of this Kingdom, we become a peculiar people, a chosen generation, and a royal priesthood. Because we are part of this Kingdom, we choose to bow and give reverence to the King of Kings and Lord of Lords! However, this scripture tells us, that whether we choose to be part of this Kingdom or not; because Jesus humbled Himself and came to the earth and suffered the death of the cross for all mankind; God has given Him a name that is above every other name. Therefore, at the name Jesus, every knee must bow, whether in heaven, on the earth, or beneath the earth. So, why not exalt the name of Jesus, willingly and reap the benefits or promises that being part of His Kingdom brings. Because whether you do so now or not, one day, your knee will bow!

Declaration and Confession:

I proclaim that I am part of the Kingdom of God. Jesus is Lord of my life. He paid a price for me and I owe Him reverence and praise. He is worthy of all honor and glory! I was captive and He set me free! Because He did that for me, I don't have a problem being subject to Him. He is the King of King and Lord of Lords. I worship Him and adore Him! I bow my will, my emotions, and my intellect to Him. He is the ruler of my life. His name is above every name that tries to keep me down. I bow my knee willingly to Him. I owe Him my very life! I believe in my heart and confess with my mouth that Jesus is Lord!!! To the Glory of God the Father!

Prayer:

Dear Lord Jesus,

Thank you for humbling yourself and leaving your Heavenly Kingdom to give yourself as a ransom for me. If you had not come, I would be eternally lost.

Gwendolyn F. Mosley

Help me to humble myself and accept the cross that I must bear, while I'm here on earth. Holy Spirit, help me to choose each day to serve the King of Kings and Lord of Lords. Help me to be aware of my own weaknesses and faults, so I can submit those areas to you. Father God, thank you for rescuing me with your divine plan and receiving me into your Kingdom. It is a privilege to be subject to you. I bow on my knees to you. You are worthy of all honor and glory. I give you praise! In Jesus' Mighty Name, Amen.

Reflection:

In what areas can I exercise more humility and even seek his wisdom in my relationship with God?

Memory Verse: John 16:33 I have told you these things, so that in Me, you may have [perfect] peace and confidence. In the world you have tribulation and trials and distress and frustration; but be of good cheer [take courage; be confident, certain, undaunted]! For I have overcome the world. [I have deprived it of power to harm you and have conquered it for you.]

Thought for the Day: "CHEERS!"

---

*D*uring a victory celebration, you may witness an individual in leadership at an event stand up and propose a toast proclaiming victory of some sort. Everyone raises their glass with their drink of choice, as the speaker gives the proclamation. Then, with a unanimous voice they all say, "Cheers!" They do this because they are excited about what just occurred or they want to give accolades to someone who has accomplished something great. They want to show their respect or give honor to someone who has overcome one of life's challenges. In our verse of scripture, Jesus is preparing his disciples for what's ahead, as He approaches His time of departure. He's letting them know that they are going to face some difficult times and He's giving them the formula for victory. If they allow the tribulations, trials, distresses, and frustrations of the world to overtake them, they will be defeated. However, He has overcome the world by depriving it of power to harm them. He gives them the key. If they will keep themselves hidden In Him, they will have perfect peace and confidence. When things get tough, they are to remember what He has already done and face their adversity with courage and confidence. There may be times when they are all alone in their circumstance or situation, but they are to remember that He is with them and has already given them the victory. These words of encouragement have been left to us, as disciples of Jesus, Christ our Lord. When we are being tried and facing times of trouble, we may feel frustrated, distressed, and stressed out! Nevertheless, we must remember that He has already defeated the world's system. No matter what we're going through, it has no power to harm us, if we remember the words of Jesus. If we remember that we are not alone, that Jesus is our conquering King. We can have perfect peace and confidence right in the middle of one of life's storms. We can raise our glass of wine (the Blood of Jesus) in the Spirit, make our proclamation of Victory (Jesus is Lord!), and say unanimously, "Cheers!"

Declaration and Confession:

No matter what this world brings my way, I have confidence in what Jesus has already done for me. He has deprived it of power to harm me and has already conquered it. Because I can depend on the words He has spoken to me, as one of His chosen disciples, I have perfect peace in the midst of trials and tribulations. Distress, discouragement, frustration, and stress have no place in me. I raise my glass in victory proclaiming, "Cheers!" to my conquering King!

Prayer:

Dear Lord Jesus, I thank you for what you have already done for me. You have overcome the world and conquered every trial and tribulation coming my way. You give me confidence and courage, when I'm faced with adversity. You give me joy in the midst of sorrow. I can be of good cheer, regardless of my situations and circumstances. You give me hope and joy, when I'm faced with possible defeat. I remember what you said to the disciples and because I am one of your disciples, I can proclaim the victory! You are Awesome and I give you All the Glory and Honor, In Your mighty Name, Jesus, Amen.

Reflection:

How can I change my perspective about my life's challenges?

Memory Verse: John 4:13, 14 Jesus answered her, All who drink of this water will be thirsty again. But whoever takes a drink of the water that I will give him shall never, no never, be thirty any more. But the water that I will give him shall become a spring of water welling up (flowing, bubbling) [continually] within him unto (into, for) eternal life.

Thought of the Day: Are You Thirsty?

---

*H*ave you ever been thirsty and you try to quench that thirst with Kool-aid, juices, or soda? After drinking those beverages, your body is still not satisfied. So, you finally give in and drink a tall glass of plain old water. Wow, the thirst you had is instantly quenched! Your body is satisfied and refreshed! That's the way you feel, when you have a longing desire for a refreshing life. It's how you feel, if life has taken a toll on you and you are all dried up and lifeless. You feel like you can't go on much longer the way you are. You want to be rejuvenated, cleansed, and purged of all that ails you. You really feel hopeless and uninspired to pursue your goals or participate in life. You're just about ready to throw in the towel. Stop! There is a solution to the way you're feeling.

The solution to the way you feel is found in these verses of scripture. Jesus has just what you need to make it through this journey of life successfully. You don't have to stay in the wilderness any longer. All you have to do is make a decision to drink from the well of living water that Jesus has for you. It's a reservoir of spiritual water (the Holy Spirit) that provides you with a source of abundant life. Your inner being is the container or well that this magnificent water resides. Once you receive this gift of life from Jesus, you can dip into this pool as often as you desire. Each time you draw from it, the dryness of life will evaporate! Simply ask

Jesus to give you the water that will eliminate your thirst and give you eternal life. He will gladly give you what you need, abundant life! The Holy Spirit will be available to you 24/7. Whenever you need refreshing, just dip into the well of living water with the dipper of God's Word. Your thirst will be quenched and your soul revived. Maybe you have already received this water from Jesus, but have been negligent in dipping into the well. Return to your Savior and ask Him to refresh your cup! He's waiting on you to return for more.

Declaration and Confession:

Lord Jesus, I receive your loving water and abundant life. I will never thirst again! I know how to stay refreshed! I will dip into the reservoir of living water by staying in the Word of God. The Holy Spirit will assist me in drawing nearer to you, so I can remain rejuvenated, cleansed, and purged. My hope is sustained and I am inspired to pursue my goals. My main goal is to please you in every way. The enemy comes to steal, kill, and destroy, but you came that I may have abundant life. I will drink from your well continually!

Prayer:

Dear Lord Jesus,

Thank you for giving me access to your well of living water. I believe that Your Word is true. You came to relieve me of my thirst for life. I want to live a life that is pleasing to you. Please come into my inner being and give me the water that will take away my thirst for ever. I believe that you have this water and I'm ready to receive it. I accept the spring of water that will bubble in me continuously and provide me with eternal life! In the Mighty Name of Jesus, Amen.

Gwendolyn F. Mosley

Reflection:

In what areas of my spiritual, emotional, and physical life do I need the Lord's refreshing? Ask Him for it now!

Memory Verse: 1 Thessalonians 5:23 And may the God of peace Himself sanctify you through and through [separate you from profane things, make you pure and wholly consecrated to God]; and may your spirit and soul and body be preserved sound and complete [and found] blameless at the coming of our Lord Jesus Christ (the Messiah).

Thought for the day: "Double Three, That's Me!"

What an awesome God we serve! From the beginning He valued and loved us so much that He made us in His own image or likeness. God is A Spirit, so those that worship Him, must worship Him in Spirit and in Truth [John 4:24; Genesis 1:26, 27]. He has three distinct parts: God the Father, God the Son, and God the Holy Spirit [1 John 5:8]. Because we are made in His likeness, we have three parts, as well:

I Am A Spirit, I Have A Soul, and I Live in a Body. Uniquely, there is another part of me that is divided into three parts, too. My Soul has three distinct parts: my intellect, my will, and my emotions. That's why I say, "double three, that's me!"

The part of me that deals with the spiritual realm, is a spirit. The second dimension of me is the soul and it deals with the mental realm or intellect, my sensibilities or emotions, and my will or decision-making segment. This is the part of me that reasons and thinks. The last part is the body which deals with the physical realm. It is the house that I live in. My five senses (touching, tasting, smelling, hearing, and seeing) function through my Body. Before God breathed the breath of life into man's body [Genesis 2:7], it was substance without life. That's why the spirit and soul of man can live without the body, but the body has to have the spirit and soul to live. Although the spirit of the male and female were created in [Gen. 1:26, 27], their bodies were not made until [Gen. 2:7; 2:21-23]. So, the eternal part of man was created first (spirit and soul). The part of us that we can see was created last.

In order to function in the earth, we have to have a body. Yet, it's the inside man that determines the outcome of the outside man. Although the spirit man is confined in the body, he should not be conformed to the body. It's the spirit man that has the opportunity to know who God is. When I accept Jesus as my Savior, the Spirit of the living God resides in my spirit man or human spirit and my spirit is born again. If I decide to make Him Lord, the doorkeeper (my will) lets my spirit man working with the Holy Spirit, the Greater One [1 John 4:4], in to override my intellect and my emotions. My body is the slave that will respond in obedience to the part of me that is in charge at any given moment. If my soul is in charge, it obeys my soul, if my spirit is in charge, it obeys my spirit. A carnal Christian is one who has accepted Jesus as Savior, but is still ruled by the soul, because my will has closed the door on my spirit man. There will be very little difference between their actions and thoughts, when compared to the actions and thoughts of a natural man. A mature Christian is one who has made the decision to allow Jesus to be Lord of their life and their spirit man is orchestrating their actions and thoughts. Their submission to the King of Kings and Lord of Lords will bring the Kingdom of God into their daily living. The Word of God is what they feast upon daily and they experience spiritual growth. So, the question is; what part of you is in charge of your life?

Declaration and Confession:

I am a Spirit, I have a Soul, and I live in a Body! I have decided to give my born-again spirit (that is working in tandem with the Holy Spirit) the authority over my soul and body. I will humble myself and submit to the perfect will of the Living God. When that is done, the enemy will have to flee from me. I will have the VICTORY!!!

Prayer:

Dear Heavenly Father,

I am fearfully and wonderfully made! You created me to be unique in the earth. Thank you for giving me the right to choose. I choose to serve you. Holy Spirit help me to keep my spirit man in charge of my soul with an obedient body that follows. In Jesus' Name, Amen.

Reflections:

Celebrate victories! Can you identify how the work of the Holy Spirit has been evident in your life? Now, take it a step further, in what facets of your life can you give Him total control?

Memory Verse: Matthew 6:33 But seek (aim at and strive after) first of all His Kingdom and His righteousness (His way of doing and being right), and then all these things taken together will be given you besides.

Thought for the Day: "First Things First!"

There are so many "things" we think we need. Of course, we have basic needs for survival. We do need shelter, food, and clothing. Most of us have these basic needs met. We may not be making the kind of income we would like to have, but thankfully we make enough to take care of these basics. We begin to have problems when we can't afford to purchase all of our wants on top of our basic needs. Sometimes we are trying to do what everyone else is doing to add to our stress levels. Or it could be that the cost of the shelter, food, and clothing we want is out of our economic range. This can throw us into worrying about money and possessions in an excessive way. This scripture passage (Matthew 6:24 – 34) tells us we can only serve one master. We're either going to serve God or mammon (deceitful riches, money, possessions, or whatever we trust in). It tells us that we need to STOP being anxious and worried about our life (what we should eat, drink, or put on).

Our concentration for life should be on the quality of life we are living based on God's standards for living. If we truly love and trust Him, then we can rest on the fact that He will make sure our needs are met. What we need to aim at and strive for is fulfilling our purpose and destiny in regards to the Kingdom of God. He has placed us on the earth for a preordained reason. Just as Jesus came to this earth to give up His life to redeem us from our fallen state, God has sent each of us here to complete a mission He has set aside just for us to do. If we focus on what that assignment is, He will take care of all of our needs and many of our wants. He will give us the desires of our heart. Our desires will line up with His desires for our life and we will be in harmony with our Creator. True satisfaction will come when we are operating in His way of doing and being right. There will be no room for anxiety or worry when we put "first things first!"

Declaration and Confession:

My heart and mind are fixed on fulfilling God's assignment for my life. I am focused on doing things His way. I am interested in being right according to God's standards for life. I trust Him to provide for every one of my needs. I believe that He will give me the desires of my heart, because my heart has His desires in it. I will not worry or be anxious about what I eat, drink, or wear. God is Jehovah Jireh my provider! If I seek His Kingdom first, all of the other "things" will be given to me besides.

Prayer:

Dear Lord Jesus,

Help me to be focused on the things that really matter for my life. I want to fulfill the destiny and purpose God has for me to complete, while I am here on earth. I want my life to count in the Kingdom of God. His way of doing and being right are important to me. Holy Spirit, I need your help in accomplishing what my heavenly Father has ordained me to do. I surrender my will and my way to you. Please give me the strength and courage I need to stay on task. In Jesus' mighty name, Amen.

Reflections:

Identify areas that may be competing for first place in your relationship with God.

Memory Verse: Ephesians 2:6 And He raised us up together with Him and made us sit down together [giving us joint seating with Him] in the heavenly sphere [by virtue of our being] in Christ Jesus (the Messiah, the Anointed One).

Thought for the Day: "I'm Sitting Up High!"

Whenever you go to a wedding reception, there is usually a special table set aside for the wedding party. It is positioned in a prominent place in the room, possibly on a little platform where everyone in the room can see. All eyes of the guests are fixed on the bride and the groom. No one wants to miss a thing that they are doing. If you have a close relationship with the bride or the groom, you may be a member of the wedding party sitting at this special table. It's your relationship with them that caused you to be chosen to participate in an event that is of utmost importance to them. You are sitting in a place of prominence, because of who they are and your significance in their life.

Well, Jesus is the bridegroom and we are the bride in God's Kingdom. Even though our own shortcomings and sin would have brought us nothing but eternal death, the intense love of God granted us His mercy through Jesus. We didn't deserve the sacrifice He made in giving up His Son, but He delivered us from the judgment we deserved to receive. Jesus was willing to lay down His life, as the groom for His bride. When He proposed to give us eternal life by the shedding of His own blood, those who accept His proposal become His bride. We accept His invitation to a new life. We are no longer condemned as sons of disobedience, chained to the prince of the air. We move from the kingdom of darkness to the kingdom of light. We get to be the other major participant at the marriage feast of the Lamb. Even while we are still in this earthly realm, Jesus has raised us up with Him and given us joint seating in the heavenly sphere. Because I'm in Christ Jesus the Messiah, the Anointed One, I'm sitting up high!

Declaration and Confession:

I belong to the Kingdom of God. I am a joint heir with Christ Jesus. He made a proposal to me and I accept it. Now, I am the bride of Christ. I will participate in the marriage feast of the Lamb. His death on the cross and my relationship with Him has given me prominence in the Kingdom of God. I now have eternal life rather than eternal death. I have been raised me up with Jesus and given me joint seating in the heavenly sphere. I am sitting up high!

Prayer:

Dear Lord Jesus,

Thank you for what you have done for me. You proposed to me and I accepted your proposal. You didn't have to do it, but you did. I will be forever grateful to you for making me joint heir to the Kingdom of God. I promise to love you, honor you, obey you, and cherish you for the rest of my life, Amen.

Reflections:

Based on your status in the Kingdom of God, are there areas of "low thinking" in your perspective about yourself and your life? How will you start elevating your thinking in these areas?

Memory Verse: 2 Corinthians 10:3 – 5 For though we walk (live) in the flesh, we are not carrying on our warfare according to the flesh and using mere human weapons. For the weapons of our warfare are not physical [weapons of flesh and blood], but they are mighty before God for the overthrow and destruction of strongholds. [Inasmuch as we] refute arguments and theories and reasonings and every proud and lofty ting that sets itself up against the [true] knowledge of God; and we lead every thought and purpose away captive into the obedience of Christ (the Messiah, the Anointed One).

Thought for the Day: "It's A Battle!"

When you enlist in the armed services, you go through intense training. The first thing taken is your personal identity. You become the property of the United States government. You are not your own. Immediately you are stripped of your civilian clothing and given a uniform to wear. Your hair may be cut to meet the regulations of the military branch you just joined. The military philosophy is implemented and you are obligated to think military thoughts. Your Commander in Chief is the president of the United States who is serving at the time you enlist. Whatever he says goes! You are put through physical training that will make you become physically fit. You are given weapons that you learn every facet about. You know about every piece and must be able to use that weapon skillfully and accurately. You report to duty when and where you are told to be. You are given all kinds of information about the enemy your country is fighting at the time. You are taught their strengths and weaknesses. All of this goes on to equip you for battle!

As quiet as it's kept, when we accept Jesus Christ as our Savior and

Lord, we enlist in God's military services or armed forces. We should go through the same type of training that our military men and women undergo in our country's military services. The first thing that needs to be addressed is our personal identity. We should be identified as a member of the Kingdom of God. Although we each have our unique personalities, gifts, and talents, we should identify ourselves as God's children. Jesus has bought us with the price of His very life and blood. We are not our own! We are given clothing to wear, as God's own chosen ones. This clothing consists of righteousness, purity, holiness, tenderheartedness, mercy, kindness, humbleness, gentleness, patience, and endurance. If we are really members of God's military forces, we need to have our mind tuned in to the higher things of God and His Kingdom. He is Our Commander in Chief! He should be the ONE giving us our strategic moves. He has provided us with armor and weapons that make us ready for battle. Our weapons are not carnal or physical. They are spiritual weapons waging war against the battle field of our mind. Aligning our thoughts with the mind of Christ causes us to pull down the strongholds in our mind. Those areas we are held in bondage due to wrong ways of thinking we have accepted through the careful strategy and cunning deceit of our enemy, Satan. We are given information about his strengths and weaknesses in our military manual, The Bible. We know that he is the thief that comes to steal, kill, and destroy, but Jesus came to give us abundant life! So, let's represent the King of Kings and Lord of Lords the way He deserves to be represented. After all, we are in a Battle!!!

Declaration and Confession:

Father God you are My Commander in Chief! I am under Your authority with Jesus leading me, as The Good Shepherd. I am Victorious because of what He did at Calvary. I accept my Call into Active Duty in Your Armed

Forces. Through the Power of the Holy Ghost, You have provided me with everything I need to Win! I am Armed and Dangerous!!!

Prayer:

Dear Father God,

I come thanking you for the privilege we have in serving in your armed forces. You are an awesome and mighty ruler! Help us to be those you have called for in these last and evil days. It is our desire to represent you well in the earth today. By the power of Your Holy Spirit, we will be the Force of Righteousness and Faith you have called us to be. In Jesus' Mighty Name, Amen.

Reflections:

How can you exercise your spiritual authority in your life today?

Memory Verse: 3 John 2 Beloved, I pray that you may prosper in every way and [that your body] may keep well, even as [I know] your soul keeps well and prospers.

Thought for the Day: "Get Your Soul Under Control!"

I used to get confused because of two scriptures that referred to salvation. One scripture said that we were saved by grace (God's unmerited favor) through our faith and that we could not receive salvation because of our own doing. It is something you cannot work for, because it is the gift of God [Ephesians 2:8]. The other scripture said we have to work out our soul's salvation [James 1:21]. I kept wondering, which is it, is salvation a free gift of God or are we to work our salvation out? The truth is we have been delivered from judgment and are allowed to partake of Christ's salvation, because we believe in what Jesus did through His death, burial, and resurrection. God has granted us His unmerited favor. Our spirit is saved, immediately. The problem is our soul [mind, emotions, and will] is still programmed by this world's system and does not receive salvation immediately. We have to renew our mind with the Word of God. We cannot allow our emotions or feelings to dictate our actions. Our feelings change from one moment to the next. How we feel depends on whether we are glad, sad, or mad; all based on the current situation or circumstance. Our will is the gatekeeper between our spirit and soul. We have to choose whether we will listen to our saved spirit or our unpredictable soul. If we choose to listen to our spirit (also where the Holy Spirit resides), then our decision will line up with what God wants for our life. If we choose to listen to our soul, we could be in trouble if it has not been redeemed. Although Jesus has paid for the salvation of our soul, as well, until we get it under control there will be a battle going on in our members. It's like the game called "tug of war." Our body is in the middle, while our spirit and soul pull us back and forth. Sooner or later one side will win over the other and our body will have to obey the side that wins. We must guard our spirit and allow it to grow to the point that it overrides our soul. The state of our body will be determined by the condition of our soul. We want to be whole beings that prosper in every way (spirit, soul, and body). We must develop or mature into spirit-filled believers. We must have the mind of Christ (be Spirit-minded). Our emotions must be controlled by the fruit of the Spirit (love, joy, peace, patience, kindness, goodness, faithfulness, gentleness, and self-control). Our will must be determined to walk after the Spirit and not the flesh. In order to carry out the plan of God for our lives and have great success, we must get our soul under control!

Declaration and Confession:

I declare today that my soul will not control my life. My spirit man is the key to my success. I am born again in my spirit, soul, and body. Because I choose to allow my spirit to override my soul, my body responds to life in a wholesome way. I am determined to walk after the Spirit and not the flesh. I choose to have great success, as I follow the plan God has for my life. My soul is well and prospers, because my soul is under the control of the Spirit of the Living God!

Prayer:

Dear Lord Jesus,

Thank for the prosperity I enjoy in every way. I am saved because of what you did at the cross. Yet, I choose to allow the precious Holy Spirit to saturate my spirit and control my soul. I am determined to walk in the Spirit and not the flesh. When you said, "it is finished" you proclaimed victory for my spirit, soul, and body. By the stripes of Jesus, I am healed and made whole. In Jesus' mighty name, Amen.

Reflections:

Lift up your soul (your will, intellect and emotions) to God. What fruits of the Spirit will help align your soul with the spirit of God?

Memory Verse: 2 Peter 1:2, 3 Grace and peace be multiplied unto you through the knowledge of God, and of Jesus our Lord, According as his divine power hath given unto us all things that pertain unto life and godliness, through the knowledge of him that hath called us to glory and virtue...

Thought for the Day: "Exercising Your Faith To Develop Virtue"

Another word for virtue is excellence. In order to have excellence, we must have faith in who God is, that He is a rewarder of those who seek Him, diligently. Our ever-developing knowledge of God and Jesus brings abundant life. Along with abundant life comes the precious promises of God. Through those promises, we can escape from the moral decay, rottenness and corruption that is in the world. Because of the lust and greed that consumes this world, we must become sharers or partakers of the Divine Nature of God. God is a Spirit and I am a Spirit, when I accept Jesus as my Savior, my spirit is "born-again". My soul and body are still dealing with the corruption of the world's system. I have to employ my spirit to override my soul (remember Get Your Soul Under Control?), so my body will follow the right Source.

None of us want to fail in life. We strive to be the best, by doing our best. In order to obtain excellence in our Christian walk, we must exercise our faith. Our divine nature gives us the ability to take what is not revealed to our senses and operate in it as fact. Because the Holy Spirit in us guarantees the promises of God, we gain courage to regulate our life by faith in God. While we are exercising our faith, we develop virtue or excellence, resolution, and Christian energy. The Word of God renews my mind and gives me knowledge about who God is. This helps me to develop self-control. Right in the middle of exercising self-control, patience and endurance will begin to develop. As we exercise steadfastness, godliness will develop. Our relationship with God the Father, Jesus the Son, and the powerful Holy Spirit makes us determined to carry out the purpose God has for our life. Our determination to live a godly life brings with it affection for those whose lives we touch. This kind of love is the unconditional, God kind of love. All of this causes us to become spiritually mature. How long will it take us to develop excellence in our spiritual walk? A lifetime!

Declaration and Confession:

Jesus came so I can have abundant life, therefore I accept my great promises. I choose to partake of the divine nature of God. I perceive, as real fact, what is not revealed to my senses, because the Holy Spirit in me guarantees the promises of God and gives me courage to regulate my life and conduct myself by my belief. I walk according to my relationship with God, not by the appearance of things. I belong to the Lord, I separate myself from contaminating and corrupting influences making me a vessel of honor, who aims at and pursues all that is virtuous and good. Because I respect Him, I conform to the will of God in thought, word, and deed. I am a born-again child of God, I love my Father and those born of Him, because I love God, I obey His orders. My work is energized by faith and service, motivated by love and unwavering hope in the return of my Lord Jesus Christ, who has chosen me!

Prayer:

Dear Heavenly Father,

I choose to exercise my faith in who you are to produce virtue in my life. It is my desire to be a child of excellence in your Kingdom. Help me to do the things that please you, so I may pursue the many blessings and promises you have provided for me. In Jesus' Name, Amen.

Reflections:

Are you having success in building virtuous character? How can you up your success rate?

Memory Verse: Matthew 11:12 And from the days of John the Baptist until the present time, the kingdom of heaven has endured violent assault, and violent men seize it by force [as a precious prize—a share in the heavenly kingdom is sought with most ardent zeal and intense exertion].

Thought for the Day: "I'm Not a Wimp!"

It is evident that we have an opponent. He is a bully and likes to hurt or frighten us, if we are operating in weakness or smaller spiritual stature. His assaults come with the intent to cause injury or damage to us in every area of our lives. He is out to kill, steal, and destroy us. So, just as a boxer enters the ring with the desire to win the purse being offered for the victory against his opponent, we must enter the ring of life determined to win the prize offered to us for being an active participant of the heavenly kingdom. Just as our opponent comes to attack with great force and becomes a direct threat to us, we must come with an eager desire to obtain the victory for the cause of Christ. Receiving the precious prize of God's heavenly kingdom for our diligence is, of course, more valuable than the prize the boxer is in the ring to receive. Our passionate quest for the kingdom of heaven brings with it a full overflowing life. That enjoyment of life comes now and throughout eternity. While the victorious boxer enjoys his prize for the moment, our rewards extend into eternity. So, just as John the Baptist took his assignment as a messenger for Christ with great fervor, we must take our assignment with the same enthusiastic diligence. He was in jail and about to have his head severed from his body, yet, his concern was if he had completed his assignment. Jesus said that there was no one born of a woman greater than John the Baptist. He was not a wimp and fought a good fight against his opponent.

His opponent is our opponent and we must fight the good fight of faith, as he did. So, I will outlast the violent assaults of the enemy and seize the kingdom of heaven by force. Because of the Greater One in me, I am NOT a wimp!

Declaration and Confession:

I will press toward the mark of the higher calling in Christ Jesus! I will receive the prize that has been offered to me. I will finish my course in victory against my opponent. His assaults will not stop me, because I build myself up in my most Holy Faith. Walking by Faith and not by sight keeps me focused and I will receive my crown of glory. The kingdom of heaven is a valuable, precious prize and I intend to pursue it until I seize it with all of the power and strength available to me. The Greater One will give me what I need to come out victoriously!

Prayer:

Dear Lord Jesus,

It is my fervent desire to receive the prize you have for me. I know the only way I can receive it is to listen and obey Your Word. I need your power and strength to win. You have given me what I need through the powerful Holy Spirit who equips me to defeat the enemy. Thank you for what you did on the cross to obtain eternal life for me. I will not shrink back from the assignment you have given me to obtain the kingdom of heaven by force. Because of what you have done for me, I am not weak, but strong. I am not ineffectual, but effective in the Kingdom of God. I am not timid, but bold in Christ Jesus. I am not a wimp! I thank You and praise You for who You are in my life. In the Mighty Name of Jesus, Amen.

Reflections:

Based on this devotional, what are you trusting God for today?

Memory Verse: Deuteronomy 28:1, 2 If YOU will listen diligently to the voice of the Lord your God, being watchful to do all His commandments which I command you this day, the Lord your God will set you high above all the nations of the earth. And all these blessings shall come upon you and overtake you if you heed the voice of the Lord your God.

Thought for the Day: "Give Me the Blessings!"

Have you ever asked your child to do something and have them respond in a negative way? Or just flat out refuse to do what you asked them? How does that make you feel? Are you ready to sacrifice everything you have to make sure they get what they need or want? Do you have a big smile on your face in delight of their disobedience? No! The first thing you think about is all the things you have done to make sure they have what they need. Then, you think about the times you went out of your way to get some of the things they want. After that, you are just completely fed up with their attitude of ungratefulness. All of the little extras that you have done for them in the past may not be available anymore. Even though you continue to make sure their needs are met, it really takes away the joy that you would have in doing so. You still love them, but you are not happy with their lack of respect for who you are in their life. You're their parent and if need be, you would die for them! Yet, they are treating you like you have no place in their life.

Even as natural human beings, we expect our children to obey us. Why? Because we care for them, provide for the, and love them. We want the very best for our children and go out of our way to make them happy.

So, when they respond to our love with bad attitudes and disobedience, we are not proud or happy parents. We're their parents because we gave birth to them. They carry our name and we want to be proud of them. What they do is a reflection of who we are. When they respond negatively, we are forced to take away the goodies that we had planned to give them. Instead, they wind up with just the mere necessities of life. This is not pleasing to us, but we have no choice. We're made in God's image and have the same desires, as a parent, as He does for our life. He created us, gives us life, cares for us, provides for us, gave His life for us, and loves us unconditionally. This scripture tells us all of the blessings that will come on us and overtake us if we are obedient children [Deuteronomy 28:1-14]. The list is long, but they all equal abundant blessings in life. Please take the time to read the whole passage. However, from [Deuteronomy 28:15-68] there is a list of curses that will come on us, if we are disobedient children. Thank God for Jesus, who has redeemed us from every curse of the law! His death, burial, and resurrection, love, and redemption help us to stay in line for the abundant blessings God has given me!

Declaration and Confession:

Lord thank you for forgiving my disobedience. My desire is to please you daily. I know I am not perfect and you have made a way, through Jesus, for me to repent and continue my walk with you. So, I receive your forgiveness and will make obedience my way of living. In order to obey You, I must know your Word and be attentive to Your Voice. So, I commit to reading Your Word daily, praying daily, and listening to Your response for direction and correction. I choose to live for You wholeheartedly and to make obedience to You my lifestyle. Lord, please give me the blessings!

Prayer:

Dear Heavenly Father,

Thank you for creating me. You bless me by caring for me, protecting me, and loving me daily. I can do nothing without you. It is my desire to bring you honor and glory, because you deserve it. I am your child and I want to please you. You cause my enemies to flee from me. You provide all of my needs. Thank you, Jesus, for dying for me, so I can have a relationship with my heavenly Father. When I obey Him and follow His directions through His Word, I am blessed. Then, I am blessed wherever I go, my children are blessed, my household is blessed, my activities are blessed, and my positions are blessed. Thank you for causing me to have great success in life. In Jesus' wonderful name, Amen.

Reflections:

Make a list of things you're grateful for.

Memory Verse: Galatians 5:16, 17 But I say, walk and live habitually in the (Holy) Spirit — responsive to and controlled and guided by the Spirit; then you will certainly not gratify the cravings and desires of the flesh — of human nature without God. For the desires of the flesh are opposed to the (Holy) Spirit, and the [desires of the] Spirit are opposed to the flesh (Godless human nature); for these are antagonistic to each other — so that you are not free but are prevented from doing what you desire to do.

Thought For The Day: "I Don't Feel Like It!"

---

*H*ow many times have we said these words to ourselves or out loud? It's extremely easy to go by our feelings at any given time. However, the Word of God tells us not to walk according to what we feel, because what we feel comes from our soul. We are a trinity within a trinity. We are a spirit, we have a soul, and we live in a body. Our soul is made up of a trinity, also. It contains our intellect, our emotions, and our will. When we respond to our feelings, we are subjecting ourselves to our emotions. Our emotions may be influenced by what we think or what we want. The I, Me, and My syndrome is in effect, causing us to walk by our senses (what we can see, smell, hear, feel, and taste).

This scripture is telling us to walk and live in response to how the Holy Spirit in us tells us to. We are to be controlled and guided by Him. If we yield what we feel to the direction of the Holy Spirit, we won't bow to the wishes of our human desires. We don't want to operate in the natural. Operating in the natural causes us to respond to the desires of the flesh. To be successful in accomplishing what God has for us to do, we must oppose the desires of our flesh. If we belong to Jesus Christ, our flesh has been crucified. The Holy Spirit lives in us. So, if we live by the Holy Spirit, let's walk by the same Spirit. Next time you hear yourself saying, "I don't feel like it", ask the Spirit of God in you how He feels. If your feelings don't line up with what He feels, cancel your feelings and walk in the Spirit instead of your flesh!

Declaration and Confession:

It is my desire to walk in the Spirit and not in the flesh. Because I have accepted Jesus as my Savior, my flesh has been crucified with Him. Therefore, I will not allow my feelings to dictate to my actions. I will be led and controlled by the Spirit of God that dwells in me. Flesh you are dominated by the Spirit in me and feelings you must line up with God's feelings and desires for my life. I will walk in the Spirit and not in the flesh!

Prayer:

Dear Lord Jesus,

Thank you for your ability to override my natural tendencies. You are the Greater One in me and I will allow you to dominate my flesh. I choose to follow you this day. I will yield to how you feel and not how I feel in every situation. Please direct my path, as I lean to your understanding and not my own. Energize me, by your Spirit, to walk with strength and determination. Help me to obey you and walk in your perfect will for my life. In the Name of Jesus, Amen.

Reflections:

What are your natural areas of weakness that cause you to rely on your feelings rather than the Spirit of God within you? Submit them to God and resist the temptation to walk in the flesh rather than the Spirit.

Memory Verse: Romans 12:1, 2 I appeal to you therefore brethren, and beg of you in view of [all] the mercies of God, to make a decisive dedication of your bodies [presenting all your members and faculties] as a living sacrifice, holy (devoted, consecrated) and well pleasing to God which is your reasonable (rational, intelligent) service and spiritual worship. Do not be conformed to this world (this age), [fashioned after and adapted to its external, superficial customs], but be transformed (changed) by the [entire] renewal of your mind [by its new ideals and its new attitude], so that you may prove [for yourselves] what is the good and acceptable and perfect will of God even the thing which is good and acceptable and perfect [in His sight for you].

Thought for the Day: Be Transformed!

When my sons were growing up, they were into toys called the Transformers. They were made out of hard colorful plastic and would start out as a recognizable object like a car or a truck. However, they had movable parts that would change into larger and more powerful looking beings. They were amazing toys that would start off as a normal toy and the creator would design them to turn into something masterful. That's how we are as Christians. We start off this life as natural human beings who are programmed by this world's system or way of doing things. During this time we function and think the way we've been taught in our homes, in our schools, in our communities, and our government. At whatever age we are introduced to Jesus as our Savior, our lives experience a great change. We go from being a natural human being to being a supernatural one. At first we have no idea what has really transpired. We still look like a normal human being, but as we renew our mind with the Word of God, something happens to the way we think. We transform from a natural human being to a spiritual human being. We are more powerful than before, because we have access to a supernatural world!

Just as the creator of the Transformer toy had in mind what he wanted his normal toy to turn into, our Creator has in mind what He has designed us to be from the very beginning of our existence. When we decide to accept His offer of salvation from this world's system, we enter into a new life with new demands. In order to transform into the being our designer intended for us to be, we have to dedicate ourselves wholly to Him by allowing Him to have access to our bodies, our minds, emotions, will, and attitudes. We become a living sacrifice to Him by pleasing Him and developing an eternal relationship with Him. We operate out of our renewed self, our spirit. We no longer listen to what the world has to offer. We are interested in what God has to give to us for a prosperous, successful life! Our desire is to be Transformed!

Declaration and Confession:

I study the Word of God daily to renew my mind. This causes me to transform from a natural human being to a supernatural one. I allow the Spirit of God to change my natural way of thinking and operating by obeying Him concerning my body, my emotions, my will, and my attitudes. God is my creator and I want to function in this life the way He designed me to. I submit to his plan for my life, because He knows what is good, acceptable, and His perfect will for me!

Prayer:

Dear Father God,

Thank you for your perfect plan for my life. You created me to be a supernatural being in a natural world. I give myself wholly to You. I want to be used by You.

Your Holy Spirit gives me the power I need to transform into who you have called me to be. Jesus is the Word in flesh. Thank you Jesus for the example you left us to follow in our transformation process. Your Word renews our mind from natural thinking to spiritual. Thank You God for receiving me as an acceptable sacrifice to you. In Jesus' Name, Amen.

Reflections:

What has God created you to be? As you renew your mind daily with the Word of God, watch God change you into the supernatural being you've been called to be!

Memory Verse: John 3:16, 17 For God so greatly loved and dearly prized the world that He [even] gave up His only begotten (unique) Son, so that whoever believes in (trusts in, clings to, relies on) Him shall not perish (come to destruction, be lost) but have eternal (everlasting) life. For God did not send the Son into the world in order to judge (to reject, to condemn, to pass sentence on) the world, but that the world might find salvation and be made safe and sound through Him.

Thought for the Day: "I Am So Loved"

What exactly does the term "so loved" mean? The amplified version tells us that it means greatly loved and dearly prized. A prize is something given to a winner of a contest. The prize itself has to be something worth trying to get. It has to be valuable enough for the contestants to want to do what it takes to get it. The participants of the contest would have to think highly of the prize. Otherwise, they wouldn't even bother to compete for it. What was the prize that God held so dearly that He was willing to give His Son's life for? It was the world, His creation. Why would He have to compete for something He created? Because the human creation He gave the power to govern or rule over the whole world committed treason against Him. There was a war going on between God and Satan (the fallen angel Lucifer). The participants belonged to two different kingdoms (the kingdom of light and the kingdom of darkness). Adam and Eve were God's human creations and belonged to His Kingdom. When they disobeyed God, they sided or helped the enemy (Satan) to gain possession of the prize. The enemy had already been judged, condemned, and sentenced to everlasting death. The only way he could get back at God was to hold hostage His prize possession or creation. God used the death of His Only unique Son, Jesus, for the ransom of His prized creation: us. Yet, He gives us a right to choose, which kingdom we want to belong to. If we choose to trust in, cling to, and rely on what His Son did for us, we will not end in destruction and be lost. If we choose the kingdom of darkness, then we will suffer the same consequence as the ruler of that kingdom (Satan). He has already been judged. God wanted His world back, so He sent Jesus to bring salvation back to His creation. He wanted us to be made safe and sound through Him! That's why I know I am SO Loved!

Declaration and Confession:

I am So Loved! My Heavenly Father loves me and considers me to be a prize worth dying for. Although I have sinned, my sins are covered with the Blood of Jesus, His Son. I am no longer rejected or condemned. Judgment has not been passed on me. Because I believe in, trust in, cling to, and rely on Jesus, I have everlasting life. I am safe and sound because of Him. I belong to the Kingdom of God!

Prayer:

Dear Lord Jesus,

Thank you for what you did for me, over 2,000 years ago. Although I know I deserved to be condemned you made a way of escape and I am so grateful that I don't have to pay for my sins. You were the ransom given to take me out of the hands of the enemy. Your love was so great that you laid down your life for me. Now, I can choose to be part of your kingdom and receive all the things you have for me. I choose you as my Savior. I love you and adore you! In Jesus' Name, Amen.

Reflections:

You are God's prized possession and He loves you so! Choose to accept His love.

Memory Verse: Psalm 25:1, 2 Unto You, O Lord, do I bring my life. O my God, I trust, lean on, rely on, and am confident in You. Let me not be put to shame or [my hope in You] be disappointed; let not my enemies triumph over me.

Thought for the Day: You Won't Be Disappointed!

No matter how close you are to other people, there's going to come a time when you disappoint them or they disappoint you. We all have family or friends that we put a lot of faith in and as humans, they fall short. Even with the best of intentions, we can give someone the wrong advice and vice versa. God wants us to develop wholesome relationships with one another. He wants us to have those in our circle that we can rely on to support us and come to our aid in time of trouble. We need encouragement from one another, so God doesn't mind if we exhort each other.

However, ultimately, there is only One God we can bring our life to and know that He won't lead us wrong. He already knows everything about us. He has an individualized plan for each one of us. He's a God of diversity, so He has the perfect road map for our uniqueness. It's a pathway set up just for us! We can trust Him totally and be confident in the direction He takes us. Sometimes we cannot understand or see the route He is using to get us where we need to be, but we must lean and depend on His wisdom to guide us. Just as a blind man has to be confident in the leading of his seeing eye dog, we have to allow God to take us in the right direction. We have to depend on His GPS (the Holy Spirit) to navigate our life for us. Unlike ourselves, family members, and friends; He won't disappoint us. He won't allow us to be ashamed of our outcome.

Sometimes people will purposely give us erroneous information. They may not have the right motive for what they do. We may even think that they're our friend or have our best interest at heart. These people may be used by the enemy to bring us harm. That's why we need to put our whole trust in God, because He really cares about our success in the earth. He uses the Holy Spirit to give us discernment, when someone is trying to mislead us. Our inner alarm system will go off, if we are depending on God. It will cause us to seek an alternate route. God always gives us a way of escape and won't allow our enemies to triumph over us. If we trust in, rely on, and have confidence in God, we won't be disappointed!

Declaration and Confession:

I trust God with my life. He has a definite plan of success for me. I won't put advice from my family and friends above the leading of the Holy Spirit. My enemies will not triumph over me! I line up my own choices with the will of God. I allow Him to direct my pathway. If I lean on Him, He won't let me down!

Prayer:

Dear Lord God,

Thank for being a dependable God! I can trust you and lean on you. You have my best interest at heart. I need your discernment to keep from listening to the wrong voice or directions. Your Holy Spirit knows how to show me the right way to go. With you on my side, I will experience great success. If I depend on you, my enemies won't triumph over me and I won't be disappointed! In Jesus' Mighty Name, Amen.

Gwendolyn F. Mosley

Reflections:

Based on this devotional entry, what are you trusting God for today?

Memory Verse: Philippians 3:12 – 14 Not that I have now attained [this ideal], or have already been made perfect, but I press on to lay hold of (grasp) and make my own, that for which Christ Jesus (the Messiah) has laid hold of me and made me His own. I do not consider, brethren, that I have captured and made it my own [yet]; but one thing I do [it is my one aspiration]: forgetting what lies behind and straining forward to what lies ahead. I press on toward the goal to win the [supreme and heavenly] prize to which God in Christ Jesus is calling us upward.

Thought for the Day: Forget About it!

O ne thing's for sure! I haven't arrived at my destination, but I'm a lot further than where I use to be! The search is still on for who I really am. The one who understands and knows the blue print of my life is God Himself! I'm making personal discoveries everyday of who I really am. As I seek the plan of God for my life, I find that it is wrapped up in the earnest deposit made by Jesus when He shed His blood for me. I belong to Him, because He paid the price of His life for me. The Spirit of God has been sent to help me along my journey in the discovery of who I am and what my purpose for being really is.

It is my true desire to carry out the plan that God has for my life. So, I cannot get that done by hanging onto what has happened to me in the past. As hard as it is to let go of things sometimes, I must release the grip I have on the things that have gone wrong and embrace the things that are going right presently. Although I have learned a great deal from my mistakes, I cannot stay at that spot in my life. I am shoving my way through the obstacles in my way to proceed to my future. The only way I can get this done without further injury to self and others is to submit to God's way of doing things. Since He has the blue print, I can save time, effort, and expense by listening to the Holy Spirit as He directs my pathway. My labor will not be in vain, if I obey the voice of God on the inside of me. I want to win the prize! I'm sure you have that same desire to press toward the finish line and crossover into Victory! This is a heavenly prize way beyond our success and prosperity here on earth. It is eternal gain. Just like me, you must forget about your past mistakes and hold tight to the core being of who God has made you to be. Strive to obtain the things Jesus paid the price for you to receive, those things that are just right for you! Grab onto your future and forget about your past!

Declaration and Confession:

I want to obtain the prize of a higher calling in Christ Jesus! I release the things of my past, whether good or bad and move forward to the things God is giving to me today. I embrace my future with great expectancy of what God has for me! The Holy Spirit will lead me across the finish line to Victory!

Prayer:

Dear Lord God,

You have the perfect plan for my life. I have missed the mark in the past and I have confessed my wrong to you. You have been faithful in giving me chance after chance to get things right. Thank you for the love that you have shown in sending Jesus to rescue me. This proves that You want me to win! So, I will let go of my past and receive what you have for me right now. In Jesus' Mighty Name, Amen.

Reflections:

Have you let go of the things in your past to pursue your future? If not, determine what they are and ask the Lord to help you move passed them so you can obtain victory in your life!

Memory Verse: Numbers 23:19 God is not a man, that He should tell or act a lie, neither the son of man that He should feel repentance or compunction [for what He has promised]. Has He said and shall He not do it? Or has He spoken and shall He not make it good?

Thought for the Day: "God Keeps His Promises!"

As parents, we sometimes make a promise to our children that we are unable to keep. When my sons were young, I tried not to make too many promises. It seemed like every time I did, I had a hard time bringing that promise to pass. Thankfully, God is a perfect parent who keeps every one of His promises! Whatever His Word promises He will do, He does. Some things He promises needs our agreement to manifest. So, if we are disobedient to what God asks us to do to receive His promise, then it won't come to pass. If we really don't believe what He is promising will come to pass, then our unbelief can cancel it out. He promised that He would never leave us or forsake us in the time of trouble. So, when trouble comes our way, we can depend on Him to be there for us. We do not need to look to everything else and everyone else to solve our problem! We have to put His promise to the test by seeking His way of escape from our problem or situation. We do that by asking Him what to do in prayer and listening to the solution He gives us. Whether we understand it all or not, we must do what He says and believe that what He said will come to pass. If we do that, He always comes through. He knows what's best for us. We may even desire a different way or method to arrive at His prescribed solution, but we must trust Him enough to agree with what He says anyway. Remember, He is not a man telling us what to do. He is GOD, our ruler and creator. What He says is TRUE! When I was unable to do as I promised my children, I had to repent to them for disappointing them. I never did it on purpose, but things would happen to cancel what I had promised. I would apologize, ask their forgiveness, and replace the promise with something else. Basically, I had lied to them without meaning to. God does not lie! What He says, He will do! If we believe and do our part, He always makes it GOOD!

Declaration and Confession:

I stand believing what God has promised me in His Word. His Word is Truth and the truth I know will set me free. I am free from worry and stress because I know God is not a man that He should lie! He carries out His promises in word and deed. I can depend on Him to bring me through ALL of my troubles. He says I am healed by the stripes of Jesus, so I am healed. He says He will never leave me or forsake me, so He is always there for me. He says I am the head and not the tail; above and not beneath. So, I am victorious in Christ Jesus! What He says for me to do, I will do. I will believe and do my part. I know my God Will Always Make Things GOOD!

Prayer:

Dear Father God,

Thank you for being a God of Promise! I can depend on you to do what you say you will do. Help me to trust you completely in my times of trouble. I know you have the answer to every problem. You are not a man that you would lie to me. I will believe what you tell me is true and accept the pathway you set for me to win. Thank you for every blessing of truth you've brought my way and every promise you've kept. In Jesus' Mighty Name, Amen.

Gwendolyn F. Mosley

Reflections:

Think about the promises God has made to you personally and according to His Word. Believe you receive them and you shall have them, in Jesus' Mighty Name!

Memory Verse: Psalm 53:1 – 3 The [empty-headed] fool has said in his heart, there is no God. Corrupt and evil are they, and doing abominable iniquity; there is none who does good. God looked down from heaven upon the children of men. To see if there were any who understood, who sought (inquired after and desperately required) God. Every one of them has gone back [backslidden and fallen away]; they have altogether become filthy and corrupt; there is none who does good, no, not one. [Romans 3:10-12]

Thought for the Day: "I Ain't No Fool!"

When I was growing up, if anyone tried to get me to denounce or go against Herbert or Juanita (my parents), I would have had choice words for them. "My mama didn't raise no fool!" They proved their love for me in many ways and one of them was to apply correction to the seat of my pants, if I tried to override their authority! God had given me to them and they made sure I had a healthy respect for who and what they represented. As a young child, I tested out this theory and they made a believer out of me. Later as a teenager (those foolish years where you think know everything and in your own estimation, have arrived), I remember being persuaded by my peers to try something they didn't agree with. I knew they didn't agree with it, but I went against my better judgment in order to fit in with my peers. When they found out, they commenced to remind me who I belonged to and exactly what that meant!

Spiritually speaking, the word "fool" connotes conceit and pride or deficiency in judgment, rather than mental inferiority. Have you ever heard the term "educated fool?" I have; that's what this meaning reminds me of. I have met people who were extremely intelligent, but when it came to making a sensible decision about everyday life, they would blow it. It would cause you to wonder where all that intelligence went! Just like I had to have a healthy respect for my parents who gave birth to me and had proven their love for me, it is necessary for us to believe that God rewards those who earnestly and diligently seek Him and develop our relationship with Him. We have to believe that He IS, that He loves us, wants the best for us, and has the best methods for us to achieve our purpose. We have to understand that without Him, we can do nothing, but with Him ALL things are possible to those who believe. We have to understand that He created us, knows all about us, and has a perfect plan for our lives. Just as that rebellious teenager, we have to come to the conclusion (after a few reminders), that we are His children and we cannot accomplish what has already been set for us without Him. He will still love us, but we cannot fully receive and enjoy the favor in life that He has extended to us until we believe in Him. We please and satisfy Him when we fulfill our purpose and destiny here on earth. Just like my parents were pleased and satisfied when I behaved as they required. We have to be obedient to God our Father so we can accomplish His very best for our lives.

Declaration and Confession:

I believe God is who He says He is! He created me and knows all about me. My purpose and destiny have already been set by Him. He has the perfect plan for my life! I know He exists, because He has proven Himself to me. I am NOT a "fool!" I understand my position in God, through Christ Jesus, His son. Because of Jesus, I have been adopted into the family of God. I am His child! I obey my Heavenly Father. I seek Him out and have a relationship with Him. I call HIM, Abba, Daddy God!

Prayer:

Dear Heavenly Father,

Thank you for creating me and making a way for me to become part of your family. I know you love me and care for me. I don't want to play the "fool." I need help from Your Holy Spirit to carry out the plan you have for my life. I want to experience great success on this, my earthly journey. I want the kind of success that gives you great pleasure. You will reward me, as I seek Your face. Holy Spirit, please help me to stay on course and not fall back into anything that does not please my Father. In Jesus' name, Amen.

Reflection:

Ask the Holy Spirit to reveal foolish ideas or thoughts that may pop up in your mind from time to time. Let Him remind you of who you are and who you belong to. Then, you can proclaim: I ain't no fool!

Memory Verse: James 4:7, 8, 10 So be subject to God. Resist the devil [stand firm against him], and he will flee from you. Come close to God and He will come close to you. [Recognize that you are] sinners, get your soiled hands clean; [realize that you have been disloyal] wavering individuals with divided interests, and purify your hearts [of your spiritual adultery]. Humble yourselves [feeling very insignificant] in the presence of the Lord, and He will exalt you [He will lift you up and make your lives significant].

Thought for the Day: Resist the Devil!

When someone is struggling with something in their life, I often hear people advise them to "resist the devil and he will flee!" Although they're accurately quoting the verse, there is one very important thing we have to do first before we start trying to resist the devil. The devil has been around for centuries and knows how to defeat us in our own strength. The Greater One is on the inside of each of us who has accepted Jesus as our Savior, so it's because of the Greater One in me that I am great! I do have the strength to resist the devil. However, I must first submit or be subject to God. That means I have to surrender myself and my problems to God. Once I run to my Father and tell Him my problems, He empowers me to stand against what the enemy is trying to do in my life. He reminds me who I belong to and the Holy Spirit stands up big in me to inform the devil of whose child I am! So, after I submit to what God is telling me to do, the devil really sees the Blood of Jesus that covers me and he has to go!

So, it's like a little child being pushed around by the neighborhood bully. At first the child tries to handle things on their own, but the bully has his way and out smarts the child. Eventually, the child gets tired of being taken advantage of and lets their dad in on what's going on. The dad tells them what they're doing wrong in their encounter with the bully. They may have been listening to their other friends on how to handle things and found out they didn't have the answer. The child apologizes to the dad and admits that he knows them better and knows how to take care of them. They admit that they should have come to their dad to begin with. The child listens to their dad, does what he says, and the bully leaves them alone. That's how it is with us. When we have a problem, we need to go to our Daddy God and talk to Him about what's going on in our life. He knows us well and will give us the exact plan we need to defeat the devil. Once His plan is implemented, the Holy Spirit will empower us to stand against the tactics of the devil. Then, our Daddy God will lift us up above our situations and circumstances making our lives as significant as He originally planned. We can resist the devil - and he has to flee!

Declaration and Confession:

I belong to Father God! He knows all about me. He has the perfect plan for my life! When the devil comes to destroy me, I go to Daddy God and get the plan of action He has for me. I implement His plan and ask the Holy Spirit to empower me to stand. With Him on the inside of me, I can resist the devil and he will flee!

Prayer:

Dear Father God,

I humbly bow before you, cleanse me of all my sins. I recognize who you are in my life. I'm sorry I have allowed the distractions of life to interfere with our relationship. I come to you with every situation and circumstance that has plagued my life. I know you are well able to do what needs to be done. Thank you for the Victory over the devil that you have given to me! In Jesus' Mighty Name, Amen.

Reflections:

Be encouraged by the times you have submitted yourself to God and remember the outcome.

Memory Verse: Matthew 6:33, 34 But seek (aim at and strive after) first of all His Kingdom and His righteousness (His way of doing and being right) and then all these things taken together will be given you besides. So do not worry or be anxious about tomorrow, for tomorrow will have worries and anxieties of its own. Sufficient for each day is its own trouble.

Thought for the Day: Worry, the Unacceptable Sin!

When we really believe and trust God, it will be evident in the supernatural peace we experience. Casting all of our cares upon the Lord will relieve us of all of our anxieties. The word "stress" would not be as active in our lives. God gives us His unmerited favor for each day, but we must trust Him to receive it. Just think about the challenges you have had in your life, up to this present time. Has God been faithful in bringing you through every problem and situation? The mere fact that He has lets us know that He will do it again, when the need arises. Although we believe that God is, if we're honest with ourselves, we don't always believe that He will do exactly what He says He will do. He makes promises in His Word and to us personally. At the time we read it or hear it, we are excited and ready to receive the benefits of it. As time passes, we begin to doubt that His promise will come true. Our doubt and unbelief manifests in our fatigue, burnout, weariness, and fainting mindset. We really begin to grieve the Holy Spirit that is in us with our imaginations working overtime with the "what if" scenarios. So, instead of seeking the Kingdom of God and being in right standing with Him, we begin to worry about the final outcome of our situation or circumstance. As a result, we are sinning against God, because we have allowed worry to become the darkroom where negatives are being developed. Let's turn the light of our salvation on the situation or circumstance and trust God's way of doing what needs to be done on our behalf. God has proven in numerous ways that He will not fail us, yet, we don't really trust Him. Trusting Him means we lean on, rely on, and are confident in Him. He is the Refuge and Stronghold of our life and we have no need to be afraid. His compassions fail not. They are new every morning, GREAT is His Faithfulness!

Declaration and Confession:

I choose not to crave and seek the "things" for my life, but will seek after the Kingdom of God and His righteousness. I trust His way of doing and being right to bring victory in every situation and circumstance I find myself in. I choose not to commit the sin of worry for my life. I trust you, God! I am leaning on, relying on, and depending on YOU! I am confident in my outcome for today and tomorrow, because I know who YOU are and whose I am. I believe what YOU say!

Prayer:

Dear Lord Jesus,

You made a way of escape for every situation and circumstance I encounter in life. If God be for me, who can stand against me? There is no weapon that is formed against me that can prosper. So, I will seek the Kingdom of God and His righteousness. Every need that I have will be met by my Father, because of You the Son, and the Spirit of God that is in me. I will cast every care upon You, because You care for me. There is no need for me to carry a load that You have taken care of. Your yoke is easy and Your burdens light. As I learn of You, the Spirit of Power, Love, and a Sound Mind will override ALL of my fears. Thank You for being a Faithful God. Help me to be a faithful disciple who does the work of the Kingdom to Your Honor and Glory. In the Mighty Name of Jesus, Amen.

Reflections:

Are there areas of worry that continue to plague your life? Cast every weight and care upon Jesus who paid the price to relieve you of this sin, because He cares for you.

Memory Verse: 2 Corinthians 1:18-20 As surely as God is trustworthy and faithful and means what He says, our speech and message to you have not been Yes [that might mean] No. For the Son of God, Christ Jesus (the Messiah), Who has been preached among you by us, by myself, Silvanus, and Timothy, was not Yes and No, but to Him it is [always the divine] Yes. For as many as are the promises of God, they all find their Yes [answer] in Him [Christ]. For this reason, we also utter the Amen (so be it) to God through Him [in His Person and by His agency] to the glory of God.

Thought for the Day: Yes, No, Maybe So!

God is not a man, that He should lie. Whatever He says, He means! The promises He makes in His Word are TRUE. He will NEVER leave us or forsake us in the time of trouble. ALL things do work together for the Good, for them who Love God and are the called according to His purpose. NO Weapon formed against us will prosper! We are the Head and not the tail. We are More than Conquerors through Christ Jesus who loves us! We are above and not beneath! Greater is He that is in us, than he that is in the world! We are healed by the stripes put upon Jesus' back! These are just a few of the yes and amen (so be it) promises of God!

If we are spiritually in tune with God the Father, we will listen to hear His voice in the answer given, when we have an inquiry. Our spirit will line up with His Spirit and the answer we will hear will always be a divine Yes! If we allow God to give us the desires of our heart and not expect Him to line up with our desires for our heart, we won't lean to our own understanding. We will acknowledge God and allow Him to direct our path. Because our motive is to please Him and not ourselves, the response we will receive will always be, "Yes!" In other words, our motive of operation must be to seek for God's perfect will not His permissive will to hear a resounding, "Yes!" He has given us the right to choose which route we want to take. If we go against His will or desire for us, we will get a check in our spirit or a no. However, we can choose to go against Him. He will permit us to choose the way we desire to go. The truth of His Word or the personal directive He has given to us is still, yes. Nevertheless, we can choose to travel down the No road. He will not condemn us, if we have chosen to make Him our Savior. The enemy will accuse us and he will convict us, but the choice is ours. God does not wonder about the correct answer to our questions, so there will not be a maybe. He will give us the way of escape or peace and safety, so we can give Him the Glory! His way or promise is always, Yes and Amen (so be it)!

Declaration and Confession:

My desire is to stay in line with God's perfect will for my life! The ears of my spirit are listening for the voice of God so I can agree with the directions He is giving me. Because I am in agreement with Him, He confirms my questions with, "Yes." If I receive a no in my spirit, I will turn and go in the direction that the Holy Spirit is leading me to go. It's Yes and Amen (so be it) for me!

Prayer:

Dear Father God,

Thank you for loving me enough to give me the correct answer to every one of my questions! I don't have to wonder which way I should go. All I have to do is listen for your voice and follow your directions. Holy Spirit, please help me to hear accurately and to obey my Father's directions. Jesus, thank you for making a way of escape for me and covering me with your precious blood. In Jesus' Mighty Name, Amen.

Reflections:

Based on this devotional entry, what are you trusting God for today?

Memory Verse: 1 Corinthians 15:45 – 49 Thus it is written, The first man Adam became a living being (an individual personality); the last Adam (Christ) became a life-giving Spirit [restoring the dead to life]. But it is not the spiritual life which came first, but the physical and then the spiritual. The first man [was] from out of earth, made of dust (earthly-minded); the second Man [is] the Lord from out of heaven. Now those who are made of the dust are like him who was first made of the dust (earthly-minded); and as is [the Man] from heaven, so also [are those] who are of heaven (heavenly-minded). And just as we have borne the image [of the man] of dust, so shall we and so let us also bear the image [of the Man] of heaven. [Genesis 1:27; 2:7, 21, 22; John 20:22]

Thought for the Day: Earthly-Minded vs. Heavenly Minded

The spirit of man (male and female) was created by God in chapter 1 of Genesis, the book of beginnings. Then, in Chapter 2, He formed the physical bodies of man and woman. When God breathed into the nostrils of the man, he became a living soul. So, we were created to be a spirit that has a soul and lives in a body. We, mankind, lived the way God designed us to live until we committed treason against God in the Garden of Eden in chapter 3 of Genesis. However, God had a plan to redeem us from the curse we put ourselves under. When Jesus rose from the grave and presented Himself before the disciples in John, He breathed spiritual life into them and said to them, "Receive the Holy Spirit!" From this experience, the New Testament Church was birthed!

After Adam and Eve fell in the Garden of Eden, they became earthly-minded in their thinking. Their soul took charge, so their mind, emotions, and will became the boss. When human beings are born into the earth's realm, we are earthly-minded. We think in line with the world's system and are natural mankind bound by the earth. Thank God, accepting what Jesus did by walking this earth, dying on the cross, and rising in victory gives us a way of escape. So, we can receive the Holy Spirit and become heavenly-minded. The Spirit of God gives light to the Word of God (the Bible) and we can renew our mind to think like God thinks. We have the capabilities to surpass the thinking of this world. We are no longer bound to this earth. We become citizens of the Kingdom of God. Even though we are citizens of God's Kingdom, we have to choose to renew our mind with the Word of God to become heavenly-minded. Otherwise, we will have the capabilities to become heavenly minded, but will continue thinking the way we were programmed to think before we accepted Jesus as our Savior. It's like an electric plug that hasn't been connected to the outlet or power source to function properly. There will not be any power going through that plug, if it isn't plugged into the outlet. Our thinking will change or the Holy Spirit will activate, when we plug into the outlet or Word of God. "Faith comes by hearing and hearing by the Word of God." Hearing, reading, and speaking the Word of God will cause our faith to grow or increase. As this growth occurs, our mind is reprogrammed, and we become heavenly-minded. I don't know about you, but I don't want to have the same kind of thinking that manifests in this world. I call it stinking thinking that is earth bound. If we choose to think this way or will to think this way, our emotions will respond in a stinking way, too. I want to think and speak God's words into the atmosphere. Because we are heavenly-minded, the words we speak, along with our actions will be godly. Then, the world will know that the power inside of us is real. Please join me and choose to be heavenly-minded!

Gwendolyn F. Mosley

Declaration and Confession:

I will choose to be heavenly-minded rather than remaining earthly-minded! I command my thinking to line up with the Word of God. The Holy Spirit illuminates my mind, so I understand the Word of God. I am heaven bound and want to represent God's Kingdom in the earth. The mind of Jesus Christ resides in me and I am heavenly-minded!

Prayer:

Dear Lord Jesus,

Thank you for coming to the earth to redeem me! Forgive me for the times I have failed to stay in Your Word, so I will display godly thinking. Holy Spirit, please renew my mind and activate God's power in me. Jesus, because You were the Word in flesh, Your actions in the Bible were not earth bound. Help me to be more like you as I reprogram my thoughts to become heavenly-minded. In Jesus' Mighty Name, Amen.

Reflections:

Allow the Spirit of God to shift your mindset, His Kingdom come, and His will be done in you today!

Memory Verse: 2 Corinthians 5:17, 21 Therefore if any person is [ingrafted] in Christ (the Messiah) he is a new creation (a new creature altogether); the old [previous moral and spiritual condition] has passed away. Behold, the fresh and new has come! For our sake He made Christ [virtually] to be sin Who knew no sin, so that in and through Him we might become [endued with, viewed as being in, and examples of] the righteousness of God [what we ought to be, approved and acceptable and in right relationship with Him, by His goodness].

Thought for the Day: God Made A Trade

---

*H*ave you ever taken the "fall" for someone else? Every now and then, when I was growing up, one of my brothers would do something wrong while my parents were gone. Because I was the oldest, I was in charge of what went on in the house. When my parents returned and the violation was spotted by my mom, she would come to me to find out exactly what happened. If I was in a sympathetic mood, I wouldn't tell her who really did it. Instead, I would take the blame for what happened. Of course, that meant that I also had to take the punishment for it, as well. I became the scapegoat for the wrong that had transpired, so my brother would get off and I would take the blame. That's what Jesus did for us. He took the punishment of eternal death, when He had not committed one sin. He took every sin that you and I have ever committed, are committing, or will ever commit; to the cross! He became the substitute for every one of our transgressions. Jesus, the only begotten son of God did that to cover the sins of ALL of His brothers and sisters. Adam and Eve fell, but Jesus took the "fall!"

Even more incredible than that is the fact that God the Father was willing to take His only begotten Son and offer Him as the scapegoat for our sins. He used His very own Son to give us an escape route to eternity. We really were doomed to an eternal hell, BUT God had another plan for the Fall of Man. He wanted a huge family. One that cannot be numbered and He was willing to plant the One Seed of His Son to bring in the harvest of an eternal family. Think about it, His earthly children messed up and handed their dominion of the earth over to Satan, the serpent. Yet, He loved mankind so much that He wouldn't allow Satan to win! He sacrificed His Son on the cross to recover the dominion lost for those who would believe and accept what His Son had done. Now, we can trade our sin in for the righteousness of God, because Jesus paid it ALL! Those who believe and receive can have dominion in the earth and right standing with God, all because God was willing to make a trade!

Declaration and Confession:

I am the righteousness of God In Christ Jesus! I believe that Jesus was born, walked the earth, was crucified and died for my sins. I believe He went into the bowels of hell and recovered the keys to the Kingdom of God. I believe that He rose in Victory and Power! I receive what He did for me on the cross! I receive the salvation that He paid the price for. I belong to the family of God!

Prayer:

Dear Father God,

Thank you for making the necessary trade for my salvation! You didn't have to do it, but You loved me enough to set me free. Lord Jesus, thank for coming and being the substitute for my sins. Without Your sacrifice I would be doomed. You deserve all the glory and praise! In Jesus' Mighty Name, Amen.

Gwendolyn F. Mosley

Reflections:

What sorrow, stress, or personal issue do you need to trade for the joy, peace and victory of Jesus and His resurrection?

Memory Verse: 2 Timothy 1:7 For God did not give us a spirit of timidity — of cowardice, of craven and cringing and fawning fear — but [He has given us a spirit] of Power and of Love and of Calm and Well-balanced Mind and discipline and self-control.

Thought for the Day: I Can't Afford To Be Afraid!

*H*ave you ever heard a creak in the night, when you were all alone? All of a sudden you get all kinds of thoughts about someone breaking in on you or walking up the stairs to strangle you. Your mind begins to race, as the flood of thoughts begin to create an end of doom for your life. When you finally stop allowing the thoughts to paralyze you, you get enough courage to tiptoe downstairs, look out of the window, and discover it's a branch from the tree that the wind has blown against the house. There is absolutely nothing to warrant the near heart attack you just experienced! That's the way fear operates. Something initiates your concern and before you know it you have heard all kinds of negative scenarios in your head. They usually start off with, "what if" or if you happen to think of a positive "yeah, but." This happens to all of us at one time or another. Although we should have a healthy awareness of things that will harm us, we should not allow the unhealthy fear or "false evidence appearing real" to overtake our sound mind. It's what we do with these thoughts that makes the difference.

One thing's for sure, you cannot operate in faith and fear at the same time, because one cancels out the power of the other. Each one is a spiritual force. Faith is a product of God's creative power, while fear is a product of Satan's destructive power. Faith comes by hearing the

Word of God, while fear comes by hearing the words of the world. Faith is developed through meditating and acting on God's Word, while fear is developed through mediating and acting on Satan's lies. Faith is applied by speaking of things that are not seen as though they were [Romans 4:16, 16] and fear is applied by speaking of things that are seen as though they will always be. Jesus is the author and developer of our Faith, while Satan supports and develops fear. In order for fear to work, you have to compromise your Faith in God. Fear is not natural to the born-again child of God [1 John 4:15-18]. Fear has to be received, before it can enter the heart and stop your faith [Mark 4:18, 19]. Fear acted on produces the law of sin and death, while faith acted on produces the law of the Spirit of Life. Faith moves God, because faith is in God. Fear moves Satan, because fear is in Satan. He cannot do anything to us apart from fear, anymore than God can do something for us apart from faith. I, personally, cannot afford to be afraid. Besides, without faith, it is impossible to please God and I want to please Him. Let's get God involved in our situations and circumstances by activating our Faith!

Declaration and Confession:

I declare that I am free from the spirit of fear! I am not timid! I have the power of God in me; the Greater One lives in me! I have the love and confidence of God in me and it casts out all fear. I will meditate and act on the Word of God. I will not compromise my faith in God. Satan and his lies will not consume my thoughts. He will not deceive me. I have the mind of Christ! My mind is calm and well-balanced. My faith in God moves Him into action on my behalf. I want to please Him! He will give me victory over all of my fears, because I trust, believe, and have faith in Him!

Prayer:

Dear Heavenly Father,

In this world, we are surrounded by all types of calamity. If we listen too long, these things can bring fear into our hearts. We know that you love us and want the best for us. It pleases you to intervene in life's situations and circumstances on our behalf. Holy Spirit, please help us to activate our faith, so God can turn things around for us. We want the abundant life that Jesus came to give us. We cannot afford to believe the lies of the enemy. Thank you for giving us the Spirit of Power, Love, and a Sound Mind! In Jesus' Mighty Name, Amen.

Reflections:

Write down scriptures to specifically combat each of your fears, then commit every fear to the Lord in prayer!

Memory Verse: Colossians 3:16 Let the word [spoken by] Christ (the Messiah) have its home [in your hearts and minds] and dwell in you in [all its] richness, as you teach and admonish and train one another in all insight and intelligence and wisdom [in spiritual things, and as you sing] psalms and hymns and spiritual songs, making melody to God with [His] grace in your hearts.

Thought for the Day: "I'm Steeped in the Word!"

The purpose of steeping your tea is to bring out the true flavor of the tea. You have to steep the tea for the correct length of time, depending on the type of tea being prepared. This infusing time varies. To infuse means to instill or impart. After you've done that, you are ready to enjoy the bountiful flavor in your cup. Whatever your favorite tea may be, there's nothing like taking the time to relax and sip on your tea. It has a calming effect on your day and may rescue you from the stress a day can bring. Steeping the Word of God in your heart and mind causes the richness of its meaning and power to bring forth strength in your life. It enhances the flavor of grace and mercy to help you to make it from day to day and glory to glory. The strength of the Word enlivens and empowers us individually and will bring insight, intelligence, and wisdom into spiritual things for us corporately. Sharing what God has revealed to us while singing psalms, hymns, and spiritual songs with one another. Praising God for what He has done for us making the melody of His unmerited favor in our hearts. This gives us insight and intelligence into the things of God. How do I know this is true? It's because I'm steeped in the Word!

Declaration and Confession:

Each time I read the Word of God I hide it in my heart, so I won't sin against Him. The longer it stays in my heart the richer my understanding, insight, and spiritual intelligence gets. Help me, Lord, to share what I receive with others through teaching, admonishing, and training what I have learned. What a privilege it is to sing praises to your Holy Name with them and to worship you with the melodies in my heart for the grace you have shown to me. I love you Lord! I adore You! I will keep your Word deep in my heart and allow it to bring forth the fruit of your love to those who touch my life. I want to remain steeped in Your Word!

Prayer:

Dear Lord Jesus,

Thank you for the Word that you have placed in my heart! It has the power to change my heart and mind. I vow to you today to read it every day, so that it can dwell in me and enlighten my thinking, in order to stay in the center of your will for my life. I want to help those you send my way to understand the grace and mercy you have extended to us. Holy Spirit, please help me to stay in the narrow path of righteousness God has for me. I praise you Lord from the depth of my soul and make melody in my heart in psalms, hymns, and spiritual songs to the God who loves me as Your Word is steeped in my heart! In Jesus' Name, I pray, Amen.

Gwendolyn F. Mosley

Reflections:

Find a new verse in scripture each week, one that may be new to you. Memorize and meditate on it as you study the Word.

Memory Verse: Psalm 34:1 – 3 I will bless the Lord at all times; His praise shall continually be in my mouth. My life makes its boast in the Lord; let the humble and afflicted hear and be glad. O magnify the Lord with me, and let us exalt His name together.

Thought for the Day: Magnify the Lord!

---

*L*ong, long ago, I remember sitting in my High School biology class where I was exposed to the use of a microscope. This device could take what the teacher placed on the glass slide underneath the lens and make it look large enough to be seen as we studied. The first thing he put on the slide was a very thin slice of onion skin, so we could see what a cell looked like. Without the microscope, we could not see the cell of the plant with our naked eye. Now that I'm much older than I was then, I use my reading glasses or a magnifying glass to make the original size of print on a page larger, so I can read the words. This is wonderful, because it helps me to enjoy and understand what I am reading.

As Christians, we magnify the goodness of God that we feel on the inside by praising Him outwardly with our voice or actions. We do this with other Believers, when we are in the sanctuary of our church. We sing praises to God, recite His scriptures together, and lift up our hands to signify our gratefulness. The question is: How do we magnify the Lord in our everyday walk in the world? The people we come in contact with on a daily basis cannot see what's on the inside of us unless we magnify what's there. Hopefully, they will see the love of God that exists in our hearts by the way we greet them. Do we show the joy of the Lord with the smile that's on our face or are we grumpy and mean as they say hello to us? Do we continue our day with positive words or constantly complain, as we encounter difficulties throughout the day? No matter what's going on, words of praise to God should be coming out of our mouth. Out of the heart the mouth speaks, so what's in our heart (the love of God) should be coming out of our mouth. This doesn't mean we have to use biblical terminology to express the God in us. It means we should have a humble attitude and reach out to help those around us, as Jesus did. People should be drawn to what's on the inside of God's people. The Holy Spirit resides in us and He has the answer to every problem mankind encounters. So, we should be people of hope and faith. We should operate in confidence, because the Greater One is on the inside of us! All things are possible; because we believe in the God we serve. As we operate in this manner, those who are afflicted can see that there is hope and a way to victory. If we lift Jesus up in our daily walk, He will draw the people we encounter to Himself. Our outward actions magnify the Lord in us!

Declaration and Confession:

I vow to bless the Lord at all times! I will praise His name, because he has done great and marvelous things in my life. I will boast to others just how great He is. I will magnify the God on the inside of me, so He can be seen by others. I am glad and His joy will be seen on my face. I choose to magnify the Lord!

Prayer:

Dear Father God,

You alone are worthy of all praise, honor, and glory! Thank you for sending Jesus, so I would know who you are. I give you my life, so You can become large in me. I want the world to know that there is a reality in knowing and serving the true and living God. I want your image to become real in me. Lord God, please magnify Yourself in me! In the Mighty Name of Jesus, Amen.

Reflections:

Name a recent or ongoing complaint you have in your life. Now, replace that complaint with something for which you're grateful.

Memory Verse: Matthew 7:1, 2 DO NOT judge and criticize and condemn others, so that you may not be judged and criticized and condemned yourselves. For just as you judge and criticize and condemn others, you will be judged and criticized and condemned, and in accordance with the measure you [use to] deal out to others, it will be dealt out again to you.

Thought of the Day: "Watch How You Judge, Reaping Is Coming!"

I learned a very painful lesson years ago. In my early adult years, I had not dated much and had a very high standard set for myself. I simply could not understand how someone could disappoint themselves and their family by getting pregnant out of wedlock. A few of my friends found themselves in this situation and I silently said to myself, "that will never happen to me." I outwardly supported them, but inside I was judging them. Well, you know what happened, a few years later I had to deal with the same scenario and I fully understood how that could happen to a person. However, I had a hard time forgiving myself for it and it took me 5 years to totally receive God's forgiveness for my transgression.

During the time of my ordeal, one of my co-workers told me openly that she could not understand how I could do such a thing to myself and my family. I told her that it wasn't intentional and warned her of my mistake in judging others for this same occurrence in their lives. She said out loud to me, "that will never happen to me, because I won't let it." Well, a few years later, guess what! There she was in that same predicament. The oldest of 11 children, she was crushed and very embarrassed. She came to apologize to me for her arrogance. I explained to her how well I understood and accepted her apology. I supported her with all my heart and told her God had forgiven her, so she should forgive herself. Mind you, I hadn't fully forgiven myself at that point, but helping her through her failure helped me to receive forgiveness for myself as well.

When you measure out judgment for others, you better be ready for what's coming back on you! ALL of us have fallen short of the glory of God. We have sinned! When it's someone else's mistake, it's hard for us to understand how they could do such a thing. Yet, when the same thing happens to us, we have all kind of excuses and mercy to offer. Or we may be like me and condemn ourselves for what God has forgiven. We are harder on ourselves and other people than God is. He loves us unconditionally and made a way of escape from every one of our transgressions. Jesus has paid the price already for what we have done or will do! We love Him, so we strive to do what's right, but in our own strength we can do nothing! So, let's recognize that we have a just judge who knows what He is doing and leave the judging to Him! Remember to watch what you judge, because as sure as you're living, reaping is coming!

Declaration and Confession:

I am NOT the judge, God is! So, I leave all judging up to Him. I will take care of the beam in my eye ONLY! For our benefit, He made Christ to be sin for us. I know if I confess my sins that God is faithful and just to forgive me and cleanse me of ALL unrighteousness. He remembers them no more! I am the righteousness of God in Christ Jesus!

Prayer:

Dear Lord Jesus,

Thank you for making a way of escape for me! I need your Holy Spirit to keep me in the right path. Help me to be careful not to judge others. I want to leave all of that up to God the Father. He cleanses me of all unrighteousness, when I confess my sins. When I fail to do what's right or have wrong thoughts, You cover me with Your precious blood. Lord, I love you and appreciate what you do for me. In the Name of Jesus, Amen.

Reflections:

Who or what have you been improperly judging? Now, find an aspect of your own life that needs work. Then, surrender it to the Lord and allow Him to mature you as you allow others the grace to grow!

Memory Verse: Matthew 5:13 You are the salt of the earth, but if the salt has lost its taste (its strength, its quality), how can its saltiness be restored? It is not good for anything any longer but to be thrown out and trodden underfoot by men.

Thought for the Day: "I Am Salt!"

Why do we use salt? We usually use it to add a desired flavor to our food. However, it is also used to preserve our foods. Have you ever heard of salt pork? It's fat pork that is taken from the back, sides, and belly of the pig and cured with salt. This heavy salting keeps the meat from spoiling. We can take strips of the salt pork and season our foods with it. In this verse of scripture, the word salt is referring to the ability to preserve. When something is preserved, it is protected from harm, damage, or saved. It means to keep from spoiling or rotting. Well, God has called us to be, "the salt of the earth," the kind of people who people consider to be the finest or best. The kind of people they think highly of. Although this is good, God is calling us to be a preservative. He wants us to keep the earth from putrefying or decaying to the point of having to be destroyed. Just as the heavy salting of the fat pork preserves it, we are to have the strength of God's Word and Spirit so strong that our presence protects and saves others.

The words we speak, along with the sprinkling of our actions, should be powerful enough to keep things from spoiling or rotting. Rather than have someone say, "I take him/her with a grain of salt," meaning they really don't believe what we have to say or doubt our ability to complete a task. What we have to say should be taken very seriously or what we commit to do should almost be a guarantee. We should be "worth our salt!" We should be worth the price that Jesus paid to save the world.

We should be valuable to the Kingdom of God. We have been called to go into the world preaching, announcing the Good News to the whole human race. Also, because we believe the Gospel we are spreading, we should be able to drive out demons, speak in new languages, lay hands on the sick and they will get well. We should be a powerful preservative to mankind, occupying until Jesus comes. I don't know about you, but I want to be "worth my salt!"

Declaration and Confession:

I am determined to be the salt of the earth! Jesus, you sent me to keep the world from putrefying. I will study the Word and allow the Holy Spirit to strengthen me, so I will be able to bring salvation to the lives I come in contact with. Whatever their situation or circumstance is, I want to be powerful enough to meet their needs. I want to be able to sprinkle your Words on the lives of people who are rotting on the inside from unbelief, so they will receive faith to live and not die!

Prayer of Faith:

Father God, you have placed me on this earth to be the salt that has not lost its ability to save. I know that I cannot accomplish this task without believing in your Son Jesus, allowing the Holy Spirit to rule and reign in me, and studying your Word. So, I commit to rely on you by applying your Word to my own life, following the footsteps of Jesus, and being empowered by the Holy Spirit. Thank You for using me in Your service, to be beneficial to Your people. What an awesome responsibility and honor. I bind the enemy from interfering with my vow by releasing the Spirit of God to have full control of me. In Jesus' Mighty Name, Amen.

Gwendolyn F. Mosley

Reflections:

Watch your words! How can you change your speech to uplift and not destroy?

Memory Verse: Philippians 4:6, 7 Do not fret or have any anxiety about anything, but in every circumstance and in everything, by prayer and petition (definite requests), with thanksgiving, continue to make your wants known to God. And God's peace [shall be yours, that tranquil state of a soul assured of its salvation through Christ, and so fearing nothing from God and being content with its earthly lot of whatever sort that is, that peace] which transcends all understanding shall garrison and mount guard over your hearts and minds in Christ Jesus.

Thought for the Day:
Supernatural Peace Is Mine

---

*H*ave you ever been anxious about something? Not in the sense of excitement or expectation, but in the sense of nervousness or worry? I have. Those times that I have been anxious are those times that I have not turned my concerns over to God. The Word says, if I make a definite request of the Lord about my situation or circumstance and release it to Him with confidence and thankfulness, supernatural peace will be mine! That means, every time the enemy comes to me with another reason to be worried or concerned; I have to continue to believe that the request I made to God was heard and the answer is on the way! I can cancel my request by listening to the thoughts of doubt that try to convince me that by request has not been heard or granted. If I really know and understand who I am in Christ Jesus and that God the Father wants what's best for me, then I can rest in His provision for every one of my needs. So no matter what state I find myself in, I can rest knowing that He will answer my request beyond my ability to think of a solution to my situation. The Holy Spirit will protect me by surrounding my heart and mind with the promises of God, just as soldiers surround a fort to keep the enemy out! If I allow these words to override the words of the enemy, I will experience the peace that only God can give. I don't know about you, but I need the supernatural peace of God to be mine on a daily basis!

Declaration and Confession:

I choose not to be anxious about anything! God hears and answers my prayers. No matter what I'm going through, God cares about me and has made a way of escape for me! Because I hand over my concerns to God the Father, His supernatural peace is mine! The Holy Spirit watches over my heart and mind to keep the negative thoughts of the enemy out. I will continue to listen to the promises God has made to me until my victory is manifested!

Prayer:

Dear Lord Jesus,

Thank you for everything you have provided me through your death on the cross. Because of your ultimate sacrifice, I can come boldly to the throne of grace and ask my Heavenly Father to get me through every situation or circumstance. When I make my request to Him, He hears me and answers my prayers. He lets me know that His Holy Spirit will protect me while I await the manifestation of His promises. I can lean and depend on Him, because You have become the bridge I need to cross over to Victory! You deserve the praise, honor, and the glory! In Jesus' Mighty Name, Amen.

Reflections:

Identify a physical place in your home or office or neighborhood – somewhere you can go and pray and meditate and allow the Lord to infuse you with His supernatural peace.

Memory Verse: Matthew 5:43 – 45 You have heard that it was said, You shall love your neighbor and hate your enemy, But I tell you, Love your enemies and pray for those who persecute you, To show that you are the children of your Father Who is in heaven: for He make His sun rise on the wicked and on the good, and makes the rainfall upon the upright and the wrong does [alike].

Thought for the Day: "I Choose NOT To Be Offended!"

O ne of the major obstacles to our faith, as Christians, is allowing offense to trap us into unforgiveness. Mind you, those who are professing children of God have problems in this area also. However, it is really sad that we find ourselves in the same position as those who have not found their connection with the blessed hope in Christ. Here we are connected to the awesome Kingdom of God and find ourselves struggling with unforgiveness, envy, and strife. All of these things lead to a root of bitterness. Let's work on not allowing the seeds of bitterness to enter into our life's picture or story.

In order to keep this from happening, we must adhere to the Word of the Living God. It tells us to do the opposite of what a natural man would do. Natural men do to others as they have been done, but the children of God should be doing unto others as they wish to be done. The Word says, "if we love those who love us, we haven't done anything." The question is: can we treat those who have stepped all over us the way we would like to have been treated? If we only reach out to those that belong to our little circle and ignore those who don't, we have not shown the love of God that is shed abroad in our heart. We need to grow and mature in our walk with God. Godliness of mind and character should be developing in us. We need to be people of virtue or excellence and integrity in order to represent Our Father, well in the earth.

Declaration and Confession:

I have been mistreated many times during my life, but from now on: "I choose NOT to be offended!" I am a child of God and He still loves me even though I have done many offensive things. Even when I was angry with Him or did not respond to His love, He loved me anyway. I choose to represent His Kingdom here on earth. I will not return evil for evil or offense for offense. I choose to treat others the way I wish to be treated. I choose to represent My Heavenly Father as I walk through this life. He loves me unconditionally and I will operate the He operates with the help of Jesus, His Son, and His Holy Spirit that is in Me!

Prayer:

Dear Heavenly Father,

You have shown me your love so many times, but I have not always done the same to those who have mistreated me. They have trespassed against me and I have not forgiven them. Please forgive me for these past actions. I want to grow up spiritually and represent you the way you deserve to be represented. Please forgive me for the times I have been offended because I felt you didn't come through for me when you were right there all the time. I need Your Holy Spirit to empower me to forgive those I feel don't deserve my forgiveness. I don't deserve your forgiveness, yet, You forgive me over and over again. I choose now to forgive everyone who has offended me in the past and ask You, Holy Spirit, to help me to forgive others from now on! In Jesus' Mighty Name, Amen.

Gwendolyn F. Mosley

Reflections:

In what area of your life have you let offense be the fence that blocks you from forgiveness and perpetual peace? Find it, name it, and make a conscious decision to allow the Lord to tear down every ungodly fence of offense and unforgiveness!

Memory Verse: John 15:4 – 6 Dwell in Me, and I will dwell in you. [Live in Me, and I will live in you.] Just as no branch can bear fruit of itself without abiding in (being vitally united to) the vine, neither can you bear fruit unless you abide in Me. I am the vine; you are the branches. Whoever lives in Me and I in him bears much (abundant) fruit. However, apart from Me [cut off from vital union with Me] you can do nothing. If a person does not dwell in Me he is thrown out like a [broken-off] branch, and withers; such branches are gathered up and thrown into the fire, and they are burned.

Thought for the Day: "I'm Clinging to the Vine!"

---

*H*ave you ever received cut flowers from a friend or love one? When they arrive they are full of life and their colors are vibrant! There is a sweet fragrance coming into your nostrils, as you breathe them in. Several days later, the color has begun to fade, the fragrance is barely there, and they're beginning to dry out. It is evident that they are disconnected from their life source. The nutrients from the soil and the water that sustained them through their root system have begun to prove their importance. You probably add some more water trying to prolong the inevitable. Yet, 2 or 3 weeks from their arrival, you will have to decide whether to discard them or hang them upside down and make a dried plant out of them as a keepsake.

These verses are giving us a similar picture of what happens to our lives when we are disconnected from the vine. Jesus is the True vine and God the Father is the one who sustains the Vine. He knows when and where to prune the vine to keep it healthy. We are the branches on the

Vine and represent the Body of Christ. As we take up residence (abide or dwell) in the Vine, He nourishes our spirit. Just as the branch of a vine cannot bear fruit apart from the vine, neither can we produce the fruit God has ordained for our lives without the True Vine. Those things in our lives that are not producing the kind of fruit God desires us to produce are cut away. Even though it may be painful and misunderstood at the time, it is necessary for us to become the kind of believers we should be. We want to be those who are worthy of representing God's Kingdom. To produce the God-kind of fruit in abundance, we must live in Jesus and Him in us. Without Him, we will look like the withered bouquet we had to dispose of from our loved one. We can do absolutely No Thing without Him! He is our source for living an abundant, productive life. So I'm going to stay connected to the True Vine and allow Father God to prune away anything that is not pleasing to Him. I'm going to be nourished by the Word of God, communicate with Him through prayer, and allow the Holy Spirit to flood my spirit in order to be of service in the Kingdom of God. I want to be one who is fruitful and multiplies in the earth. Producing the kind of fruit my Father can be proud of. I don't know about you, but I'm clinging to the Vine!

Declaration and Confession:

Lord Jesus, You are the Vine and I am the branch. I am your disciple and I want to produce abundant fruit of the Spirit. I will do this by studying the Word of God on a daily basis. Father God, prune me where I need to be pruned. Take away everything in me that does not represent your kingdom well. Flood me with the Living Water of Your Spirit, so I can produce abundantly. Dwell in me and I will dwell in YOU. I am clinging to YOU, Jesus!

Prayer:

Dear Lord Jesus,

Thank You for living in me, as I live in You. You are the Greater One in me. The seed of Your Word is planted in me and I desire to manifest Your fruit, as Your branch. Thank you, Father God, for cutting away dead, unproductive, and stifling weeds in me. Holy Spirit, please produce Your life in me. In Jesus' Mighty Name, Amen.

Reflections:

Ask the Father what Fruit of the Spirit in you needs to be cultivated more. Once He shows you, allow the Holy Spirit to water and give that fruit exactly what it needs to yield bigger and better fruit.

Memory Verse: Jeremiah 33:2, 3 Thus says the Lord Who made [the earth], the Lord Who formed it to establish it— the Lord is His name. Call to Me and I will answer you and show you great and mighty things, fenced in and hidden, which you do not know (do not distinguish and recognize, have knowledge of and understand).

Thought for the Day: Call Me!

How often have you been in a situation and picked up the phone to call a friend? You probably can't count all the times that has happened in your life! You call one friend and they don't answer. You call another one and they are busy. You call another and they say they will call you back. You jump in your car and no one is home. So, after several tries, you give up and go into prayer. Well, what has happened here? When you're in desperation, it comes down to prayer. This is our last resort. When ALL else fails, PRAY!

Actually, prayer should be the first thing we decide to do. The God who made heaven and earth, the one who formed the world and set it in motion, the One who brought everything that is into being, says "Call Me!" (Jeremiah 33:3; Psalm 86:7) He promises to answer us and show us great and mighty things! He not only promises to answer, He's the One with the plan. When we call our friends, they may answer, but they're just like us. They don't always have an answer. They may give us some advice or tell us what they think, but the One who has the most accurate answer is God! He's going to show us great and mighty things. In other words, He's going to give us solutions to our problem that we could never come up with on our own. No human being could come up with it. He has answers that are protected and saved just for our use. They are answers that have to be revealed to us, because they are things that are not in our view. We can't see them with our natural eye, because they are hidden from our carnal thinking and way of doing things. So, to get these solutions, we have to go into our secret closet, pray, and listen for an answer. This takes time and consideration. Consider who it is that has the answer. It's not our best earthly friend. It's our best heavenly friend! He has the answer to every problem that comes our way. If we would consult Him first, we would not get into a state of desperation. We would be confident that we have the answer. It's like being given an open book test. You have the test questions in front of you, but all you have to do is open up the book, read, and locate the answer. We have the Word of God to consult! It's like having a pop quiz, but the answer key has also been given to you. Things happen without warning and when they do, we can immediately call the One who has the answers to every question on the test! There is No Failure in God! We may not understand the purpose of the test we're going through, but we know who has the answers to the test. We know that He will show us the reason for the test in due time. All we have to do is go to Him and find relief from our situation! All we have to do is do what He says, "Call Me!"

Declaration and Confession:

Things happen in my life and when I don't know what to do, I will call on the only One who has the answer to my problem or situation. I can rely on Him, because He has the key to success for my life. I know He sees things in a way that I can't understand. He will give me divine revelation and show me great and mighty things. I can depend on Him and all I have to do is Call Him!

Prayer:

Dear Father God,

Thank you for all you do to keep me safe and deliver me from every adverse situation I face in life. I am confident that you have access to the perfect way of escape for the difficulties that come my way. You reveal every answer I need to solve every problem. I can pass every test, because You simply say, Call Me! In Jesus' mighty Name, Amen.

Reflections:

Are you guilty of waiting until there is nothing else left for you to do, before you decide to give God a Call? Don't wait until the last minute any longer! Vow to call Him immediately from now on.

Memory Verse: Psalms 139:13 – 17 For You did form my inward parts; You did knit me together in my mother's womb. I will confess and praise You for You are fearful and wonderful and for the awful wonder of my birth! Wonderful are Your works, and that my inner self knows right well. My frame was not hidden from You when I was being formed in secret [and] intricately and curiously wrought [as if embroidered with various colors] in the depths of the earth [a region of darkness and mystery]. Your eyes saw my unformed substance, and in Your book all the days [of my life] were written before ever they took shape, when as yet there was none of them. How precious and weighty also are Your thoughts of me, O God! How vast is the sum of them! (Proverbs 23:7)

Thought for the Day: Fearfully and Wonderfully Made!

The controversy continues in regard to abortion. This is a very sticky subject and is often voted on around the country. Women are fighting for the right to abort the baby (fetus) in their womb depending on the circumstances that surround the conception process. Is it the right of the woman to choose what should be done to her body or the right of a child to be born? Who is responsible for life to begin with? How did the woman obtain her body? Should it be called murder before or after the birth of a child? Whose freedoms are really being violated? How will these actions be judged? Who will be judged for these actions? Who has the right to judge? These are just some of the questions that we need to think about. However, this particular scripture tells us that God is responsible for forming us in our mother's womb. We are not an accident, because God has given great thought about who we are and what we are to accomplish while we are in the earth. His desire for our destiny has already been set by Him, before we are born. We can only praise and worship Him for the miraculous event of birth!

Although the workings of our very being are intricate, causing us to be fearfully and wonderfully made, how we feel about who we are can make a huge difference in what happens during our life. God has a wonderful plan for each of us, but our right to choose can make or break His plan. The choices of those who conceive us play a monumental part in our beginning advantage or disadvantage in life. Yet, I'm so glad that Our God is Awesome and can turn evil to good, if we let Him. The right to choose is ordained by God. Hopefully, we consider what lines up with His plan and what doesn't, before we choose. However, He has taken our human frailties into consideration. So, He gives us chances to repent (change our minds and perspectives) and start over. Because of His sacrifice of Jesus, there is a way out of our troubles. Hopefully, we won't allow the opinions of others to cause us to belittle who we really are. We must look at ourselves through the eyes of the Creator of life to get an accurate read on who we are. We need to think about ourselves like He thinks, because what we think in our heart determines who we believe we are. I want God to search my heart, so my thoughts will line up with His. Then, I can say with confidence, "I am fearfully and wonderfully made!"

Declaration and Confession:

I am fearfully and wonderfully made! God has a good plan for my life. I will listen to what He has to say about who I am. His thoughts of good for my life are too numerous to count! I will not listen to anyone else. My own thoughts must line up with His. I want to carry out His plan for my life! I am who God says I am!

Prayer:

Dear Father God,

Thank you for the privilege of being born into the earth! I did not bring myself here. You ordained that I be born. No matter what happened during my conception, I give you permission to take over my life. Help me to see myself the way you do. I want the thoughts in my heart to line up with yours. I believe I am fearfully and wonderfully made! In Jesus' Mighty Name, Amen.

Reflections:

Who has God made you to be? If you don't know, ask Him who you are in Christ Jesus and listen to what He says.

Memory Verse: Philippians 4:8, 9 For the rest, brethren, whatever is true, whatever is worthy of reverence and is honorable and seemly, whatever is just, whatever is pure, whatever is lovely and lovable, whatever is kind and winsome and gracious, if there is any virtue and excellence, if there is anything worthy of praise, think on and weigh and take account of these things [fix your minds on them]. Practice what you have learned and received and heard and seen in me, and model your way of living on it, and the God of peace (of untroubled, undisturbed well-being) will be with you.

Thought for the Day: Fix Your Mind On This!

I don't really think we get just how powerful and important our thought life is. There is a saying, "You are what you eat." This speaks to the need for us to watch what we eat to maintain good health. Although this statement is true and worthy of attention, we need to take these verses of scripture to heart, too. These verses of scripture are really telling us that what we think affects our life-style or way of living. So, how we think affects every area of our life, from what we eat to what we emotionally and spiritually consume.

Thinking on the things that are true brings freedom into our living. If we are not believing the lies of the enemy, we are listening to the right voice. God is a God of truth! We can trust what He has to say. Because we have deep respect for God and love Him, we will obey His instructions for our life and honor Him with the way we live. Our awe for who He is and genuine love for Him causes us to live a life of purity. We allow the Holy Spirit to cleanse our hearts and minds. So if we are allowing the

Holy Spirit to take charge, we will be attractive to others. Our kindness will draw those who are hurting and our life-style will be an example of God's grace working in us. We will be people who praise the activity of God in our lives rather than being the kind of people who complain, moan, and groan all the time. Our pleasant attitudes will bring out the excellence of moral character that we have on the inside. This goodness and love that God has placed in our hearts will cause us to treat ourselves and others right. If we treat ourselves right, we will be conscious of what we eat, drink, and think. We will operate in a way that brings wholeness to our life; spirit, soul, and body. Living this kind of life takes away the destructive things that bring trouble and misery our way. We can enjoy supernatural peace! I don't know about you, but I want to be free, so I'm going to fix my mind on these things!

Declaration and Confession:

I choose to think good thoughts! I will not believe the lies of the enemy! Because I think on those things that are true, I am free! The truth of God I know sets me free! I choose to live a life that honors the God I serve! I am an example to others, so I model the correct way of living. The Holy Spirit gives me the power to live right. I cast down the thoughts that are not honorable to God. I fix my mind on the things above!

Prayer:

Dear Father God,

I want to honor you with my life! I can't do this on my own, so I need the Holy Spirit to spotlight the things I need to keep my mind on. He will show me the things that don't belong. I will pattern my living by the way Jesus operated, when He was here. His Word tells me what I need to do. I will fix my mind on the things that are true. The truth that I know will keep me free. I know Jesus gave His life for me, so I can live with You through eternity. Thank You for never leaving me! You give me peace. In Jesus' Mighty Name, Amen.

Reflections:

What have you been fixing your mind on? What are your thought patterns? Weight your thoughts and determine what is weighing you down. Cast down any thoughts that are trying to become a stronghold in your life, in Jesus' Mighty Name!

Memory Verse: Numbers 13:30 – 33 Caleb quieted the people before Moses, and said, Let us go up at once and possess it, we are well able to conquer it. But his fellow scouts said, We are not able to go up against the people [of Canaan], for they are stronger than we are. So they brought the Israelites an evil report of the land which they had scouted out, saying, The land through which we went to spy it out is a land that devours its inhabitants. And all the people that we saw in it are men of great stature. There we saw the Nephilim [or giants], the sons of Anak, who come from the giants; and we were in our own sight as grasshoppers, and so we were in their sight. (Numbers 14:8, 9)

Thought for the Day: I Am NOT a Grasshopper!

Out of the 12 spies that were sent into the Promised Land, only two of them, Caleb and Joshua came back with a good report. How we see ourselves when we are challenged by life makes a big difference in our outcome. The ten spies saw themselves defeated before they even got started. They told Moses that this was a good land filled with milk and honey. They even brought back some of the excellent fruit in the land. Yet, they continued to believe that they were mere grasshoppers in their own sight. Just think about that, a regular-sized man would have no problem squishing a grasshopper, not to mention a giant! They really minimized themselves to zero. They discounted everything God had done for them to get them out of Egypt and began to grumble, requesting to return to bondage. God's ability to sustain them all along the way had been proven over and over again. Instead of praising Him, they were cursing Him with their attitude and mouth. How many times have we been guilty of the same thing? God gets us out of jam after jam, but every time we encounter a new challenge we whine, moan, and groan. We give Him no credit for His ability to defeat the giants in our lives. We speak out our fears and doubts, instead of our faith and power to overcome. These doubters forced Moses to go to God and plead for mercy.

Not only did they see themselves as grasshoppers, they proclaimed that the people of Canaan also saw them as grasshoppers. Since they were spying out the land, it was very possible that the people of Anak didn't even get to see them to form an opinion. The devil is a liar! He can have us so full of fear that we project our own feelings of doubt and unbelief onto our enemies. We will look at our inadequacies and say that other people see us that way and they haven't even thought about us one way or the other. I've had people say that I think I'm something above who they are and I was busy trying to take care of my business without them even on my mind. We've got to stop counting on who we think we are and realize that with God on our side, "We are well able to conquer the giants that come against us!" Without God, we can do NO Thing, but with God on our side, ALL Things are possible to them that believe!

Because of their attitudes, grumbling, and complaining; God had to cancel His promise to take the Israelites into the Promise Land. Even with Moses and Aaron pleading their case, God had had enough. He only permitted Caleb and Joshua, along with their families to enter the Promise Land. All the descendants of the grasshoppers (20 and over) died in the wilderness over a 40 year period (interestingly, one year for each of the 40 days they were given to spy the land). Caleb and Joshua believed that they could do ANYTHING with God on their side! Because of their trust in God, not themselves, they were victorious! We have the same options in every challenge that we face. We can choose to fall under the curse or we can choose to accept the blessings God has in store for us.

Looking at ourselves without God, we may appear to be a grasshopper. I choose to look at myself WITH God, so I Am NOT a Grasshopper!!!

Declarations and Confessions:

With God on my side, I am More than a Conqueror! When challenges come my way, I trust in the God who has provided a way of escape many times before. There is NO Thing too hard for My God! I Am NOT a Grasshopper!

Prayer:

Father God,

Please forgive me for all of the times I have doubted your abilities and have tried to depend on mine. Without you, I am defeated before I get started, but with You, I can do ALL things through Christ who strengthens me. Thank you for being there for me in every challenge I face. You have given me the ability to defeat every giant that comes my way. Thank You Lord, for your supernatural way of escape! In Jesus' Mighty Name, Amen.

Reflections:

Do you see yourself as the victim or the victor? Are you overwhelmed by the situations and circumstances in your life? Know that your God is big enough to kill any giant in your life. You're NOT a grasshopper!

Memory Verse: 2 Corinthians 12:8-10 Three times I called upon the Lord and besought [Him] about this and begged that it might depart from me; But He said to me, My grace (My favor and loving kindness and mercy) is enough for you [sufficient against any danger and enables you to bear the trouble manfully]; for My strength and power are made perfect (fulfilled and completed) and show themselves most effective in [your] weakness. Therefore, I will all the more gladly glory in my weaknesses and infirmities, that the strength and power of Christ (the Messiah) may rest (yes, may pitch a tent over and dwell upon me! So for the sake of Christ, I am well pleased and take pleasure in infirmities, insults, hardships, persecutions, perplexities and distresses; for when I am weak [in human strength], then am I [truly] strong (able, powerful in divine strength).

Thought for the Day: Let the Weak Say, I Am Strong!

There was a children's song that we use to sing, when I was little. The words were:

Jesus loves me! This I know;

For the Bible tells me so.

Little ones to Him belong;

They are weak, but He is strong.

As a little child, we use to sing this with all our might!

Yes, Jesus loves me;

Yes, Jesus loves me;

Yes, Jesus loves me;

For the Bible tells me so!

*I*f we could just believe these words with all the fervor that we sang these words, we would truly endure the attacks of the enemy. He uses infirmities, insults, hardships, persecutions, perplexities, and distresses to get us to lose our confidence in the fact that Jesus loves us and gave His life for us to be victorious! God's favor, loving kindness, and tender mercy will see us through ALL of our adversities!

In a contemporary song written by my son, Kenneth, the words are:

> My GRACE is sufficient,
> What I put in you defeats what's pursuing you;
> Seek my face, rest in my Glory,
> For My Grace, Grace is sufficient for You!

This song emphasizes that God, through the Holy Spirit that is in us, has placed in us what we need to defeat whatever the enemy is using to knock us out. It is true that in our own strength we are weak, but the strength of God is in us to bring Victory our way. We have divine strength that makes us powerful and able to win the battle. Actually, the battle is not ours, it's the Lord's! So, if we seek the face of God for direction and use His strategies, we will come out on top in the end. Therefore, we can be like Paul and realize that the times we find ourselves being challenged in life are the opportunities for God to show up and proclaim His strength through our weakness. I Am that I Am is in us and what follows I Am is who we really are. Then we can say with confidence, "Let the weak say, I AM Strong!" (Joel 3:10)

Declaration and Confession:

I AM Strong! Because of the Spirit of God that is in me, I can do all things through Christ who strengthens me! God's unmerited favor, mercy, kindness, and unwavering love has been extended to me. No matter what's going on in my life, I have the Victory!

Prayer:

Dear Lord Jesus,

Thank you for the grace you have provided for me. I have not earned it, but You paid the price for me to receive it. Your divine favor is needed and necessary for me to experience the victory in this life. Thank you for loving me so! In Jesus' Mighty Name, Amen.

Reflections:

Are you trying to do things in your own strength? If so, let God's unmerited favor cancel out your natural strength and replace it with His supernatural power!

Memory Verse: Isaiah 54:17 But no weapon that is formed against you shall prosper, and every tongue that shall rise against you in judgment you shall show to be in the wrong. This [peace, righteousness, security, triumph over opposition] is the heritage of the servants of the Lord [those in whom the ideal Servant of the Lord is reproduced], this is the righteousness or the vindication which they obtain from Me [this is that which I impart to them as their justification], says the Lord.

Thought for the Day: No Weapon Shall Prosper!

As much as I would like to think that I am loved by everyone, I know that's not true. There are those who are out to do me harm. There are those I don't even know, who may be used by the enemy to bring calamity my way. I've been lied on before and mistreated. I've been looked over or by-passed for a position I thought I deserved. My intentions may have been taken wrong. There have been times that I felt all alone. All of these things come along with the package we call life. None of us are exempt from having hard times. We've all been misunderstood. There are times that we have even disappointed ourselves, not to mention those who are dear to us. Thank God, we have a heavenly Father who can make everything alright. He really has our back!

I remember going in to exonerate our sons for an unjustified wrong. As parents we did everything we could to protect our children. We really didn't want them to experience the hurts we had encountered in life. We tried our best to prepare them for life's disappointments. Although we were able to keep some of these things out of their experiences as children, we couldn't keep life's difficulties away from them forever. There came a time for each one of them that we couldn't do a thing to take away the pain they had to experience. Each one of them had to make their own choices and decisions. They had to suffer the consequences or enjoy the victories. They have had relationships that have blessed their lives and those that have caused them pain. They've had to deal with the loss of friendships or loved ones. Even though we may have given them support or encouragement, we really couldn't supply everything they needed. We couldn't stop the wrong that has come their way. They've had enemies we could not eliminate from their lives. However, what they did have was access to the same God! He knows how to take every weapon that is formed against us and use it for our good. Those words that have been spoken against us have not accomplished what they were sent to do. He's able to bring victory out of defeat! He knows how to bring peace, security, and triumph in the midst of our opposition. Because we are servants of the Most High God, we are vindicated! The Blood of Jesus covers our sins and justifies us! Even when we are guilty, our confession and repentance grants us forgiveness. No matter who or what the enemy sends our way, if we trust God, we'll be alright. Our God makes the difference in our lives. We can rest assured that NO weapon formed against us shall prosper!

Declaration and Confession:

No weapon formed against me shall prosper! I am a child of God. He has my back! When the enemy comes against me, He will have to stand against the Most High God who is the head of my life! Every ungodly word spoken against me must fall to the ground. Peace and safety belong to me!

Prayer:

Lord God, thank you for providing the protection I need to be successful in life. The assignments of the enemy against my life are cancelled! I have victory over every negative word spoken against me. I know you have my back! Holy Spirit, please erase the effects of every instance of pain I've had to endure. No weapon formed against me shall prosper. Jesus is Lord of my life! In Jesus' Mighty Name, Amen.

Reflections:

The fiery darts of the enemy may fly, but the shield of your faith in God will quench them every time you activate the shield. So, proclaim, "No weapon formed against ME will prosper!"

Memory Verse: 1 John 4:1 – 3 Beloved, do not put faith in every spirit, but prove (test) the spirits to discover whether they proceed from God; for many false prophets have gone forth into the world. By this you may know (perceive and recognize) the Spirit of God: every spirit which acknowledges and confesses [the fact] that Jesus Christ (the Messiah) [actually] has become man and has come in the flesh is of God [has God for its source]: And every spirit which does not acknowledge and confess that Jesus Christ has come in the flesh [but would annul, destroy, sever, disunite Him] is not of God [does not proceed from Him]. This [non-confession] is the [spirit] of the antichrist, [of] which you heard that it was coming, and now it is already in the world.

Thought for the Day: Put It to The Test!

*T*his is one scripture that every Believer needs to understand and memorize. I had been a Christian for two decades before I was shown this important passage. The Holy Spirit gives us the ability to discern the spirits as to whether they are of the enemy or of God. If we get a check in our spirit, there's probably a good chance something is not right. It's like a little alarm that goes off on the inside of you. It can happen when you're talking to someone or something that's being said that doesn't sit right with you. It can just be something you feel in the atmosphere. While we cannot solely rely on hunches or feelings, this scripture is a sure fire way to check out what you're getting when you're asking a question.

You may be praying about what you should do about something. You perceive an answer that could be right or could be wrong. It's not something that is in direct opposition to the Word of God. If what you are getting for an answer is in direct opposition to the Bible, it's definitely the wrong choice. You can use this scripture to test what you are getting. When each of our sons were trying to decide which college they should go to, we ran this test. They took the choices they had been offered or accepted to, regardless of scholarship or not, asking the Lord if this was the school they should go to and waited for an answer. Once they got an answer they used this scripture to test it. They asked: Do you believe that Jesus was born into the earth as a man, was crucified and died on the cross, was buried and rose from the grave? If they got an answer of "yes," their answer was of God. If they got a "no" or silence, their answer was not of God. To further safeguard this important question, my husband and I went through their choices and ran the same test. Once every one had their answer, we compared what we got. Amazingly, our answers all matched. So, we were confident in their choice for school. It doesn't matter if it's something extremely important or just something you need simple direction on. This test has been placed in the Bible for us to use. Isn't it wonderful that God cares about everything that concerns us! There's nothing too big or small, He cares about it ALL!

Declaration and Confession:

I belong to God! He cares about the decisions I make. He doesn't want me to be led wrong. So I try the answers I get to make sure they are of God. I will not allow any spirit that is anti-Christ to trick me! I put my faith in God! If the spirit believes that Jesus, the Messiah, came in the flesh, it is of God!

Prayer:

Dear Lord God,

Thank you for loving us enough to set up a safeguard for us to use! We need to know who we are getting our directions from. I feel secure in knowing that I can use this test to make sure I'm listening to the right source. You are the only source I need in order to stay on the right path. Your Spirit on the inside of me gives me the spiritual alerts I need and I am thankful that I have discernment. Jesus came to rescue me from the grip of the enemy and his cohorts, so I am grateful that He arose from the grave in Victory! Please make this scripture come alive in my prayer life. In Jesus' Mighty Name, Amen.

Reflections:

Have you received an answer you're not sure about? Take the time to test it and see what you get. Remember, a definite "no" or silence means your answer is not of God. A "yes," sometimes accompanied by an explanation means your answer is good to go.

Memory Verse: Luke 6:46-49 Why do you call Me, Lord, Lord, and do not [practice] what I tell you? For everyone who comes to Me and listens to My words [in order to heed their teaching] and does them, I will show you what he is like. He is like a man building a house, who dug and went down deep and laid a foundation upon the rock; and when a flood arose; the torrent broke against that house and could not shake or move it, because it had been securely built or founded on a rock. But he who merely hears and does not practice doing My words is like a man who built a house on the ground without a foundation, against which the torrent burst, and immediately it collapsed and fell, and the breaking and ruin of that house was great.

Thought for the Day: Not by the Hair of My Chinny, Chin, Chin!

*T*his scripture reminds me of the story about the Three Little Pigs! We are just like those pigs. Two out of the three pigs wanted the benefit of building their house to stand against the hot air of the Big Bad Wolf, but they didn't want to do the work that was required to bring about safety when peril struck their house. That's just about how we are. We call on the Lord in our distress and He gives us everything we need to build our life on a solid foundation. He saves us from death, hell, and destruction, because all we have to do is call on the Name of the Lord and we are saved. So, we call on the awesome Name of Jesus, accept Him into our heart, and we're just as happy as we can be! We are told by the man or woman of God to get into the Word of God so our foundation will be strong and able to withstand the test of time. At first we are excited and we gladly do just that! We are at the church house every time the door is open. We access the Word while we are present, but never get into it on our own. But life happens, and we soon start making excuses for missing services and Bible classes. Before we know it, we are too tired to attend church, even once a week on Sunday. We find ourselves flipping on the TV to catch a little bit of what's on Christian programs. We have no accountability to God or man, and soon fall totally out of fellowship with either one. So, when calamity slams against our life, we are scrambling around trying to find safety in the midst of our storm.

We can choose to be like the one pig who built his house on a sure foundation and took the time to use the proper materials to produce a dwelling that could withstand the violent winds of life. While everyone else decided to play around and depend on the study of someone else, he was busy getting into the Word daily for himself. He dug deep into the treasures within the Bible to develop his relationship with the Rock of his salvation. He allowed Jesus to fill him with the Holy Spirit and practiced daily communication with the One he loved. He did not take his relationship for granted and assembled himself with the saints of God. He had the support and encouragement of those who were determined to exercise their faith in a God who had proven Himself over and over again. They shared their words of testimony with him and he was secure in whom he believed. So, when the violent winds hit his life, he was able to proclaim that the Big Bad Wolf had no power over him! No matter how hard he huffed or puffed, he could not blow down the house of this Believer. The revelation of who Jesus was and who he was in Jesus was solid!

That's really how we want to be. We want to dig deep and build our life on the Rock of Jesus Christ! We want to get into the Word of God and study, so we will not have to be ashamed. We want to open our hearts up to the Spirit of God so He can overflow in us and we will have the power to stand against the wiles of the devil. We want to have fruitful communication on a daily basis to develop our relationship with God the Father, Son, and His Holy Spirit. Then, when the storms of life hit our life (and they will hit) and it seems as if the voice of fear and doubt says what that age old Big Bad Wolf said, "I will huff and puff and blow your house in," we will be able to say with confidence, "Not by the hair of my chinny, chin, chin!"

Declaration and Confession:

I am determined to build my life on the solid Rock of Jesus Christ, my Lord! I study the Word of God and hide it deep within my heart. I am a hearer and a doer of what God says. I have the Victory over every storm that comes my way. I shall not be moved!

Prayer:

Dear Lord Jesus,

Thank you for being the solid Rock in my life! I cannot make it without you. I hide Your Word in my heart, so I will not sin against You. I love You Lord and I lift my voice to worship You! You bring Victory my way in the time of storms. I appreciate You and adore You! All other ground is sinking sand. In Jesus' Mighty Name, Amen.

Reflections:

You may feel like the devil is trying to blow your house down! Stand still and see the salvation of the Lord, because you are secure - if you're standing on the Rock!

Memory Verse: Matthew 12:43 – 45 But when the unclean spirit has gone out of a man, it roams through dry [arid] places in search of rest, but it does not find any. Then it says, I will go back to my house from which I came out. And when it arrives, it finds the place unoccupied, swept, put in order, and decorated. Then it goes and brings with it seven other spirits more wicked than itself, and they go in and make their home there. And the last condition of that man becomes worse than the first. So also shall it be with this wicked generation.

Thought for the Day: Swept Clean

*H*ave you ever seen a person receive prayer for deliverance or healing and then several months later they are in worse shape than before? This is a very important discussion that we need to consider. Many times we are so anxious to help someone be set free or healed in that moment, that we forget to emphasize the need for them to fill themselves with the Word of God and His Spirit. It thrills us to see someone in bondage be set free! Everyone cheers and celebrates when this happens. We should be excited and thrilled because the Spirit of God has done a magnificent thing through the human vessel that has been used. The power of God has been displayed, which encourages us. It confirms the fact that we serve a living God who has the power to set His people free!

Sometimes, when Jesus set someone free, He also said, "Go and sin no more!" He was warning them that they were obligated to stay clean by staying away from the sin that got them in that condition in the first place. However, to remain free they had to employ what got them free. It was the Word of God and the ways of God that freed them. In the spitting incident with the man born blind (John 9), Jesus said, the man nor his parents had sinned, because the purpose for his blindness was to bring God glory. He later found the man who was being questioned by the leaders of the church and asked him if he believed in the Son of God. When the man understood who he was talking to, he cried out "Lord, I believe!" He became a follower of Christ. Whether the condition of a man in bondage is due to his own sin or for the workings of God to be manifested, Jesus must be acknowledged as the source of deliverance! The individual must confess who God is through the Word of God and by the Holy Spirit. The space that has been vacated must be filled. This is an important aspect of deliverance. The enemy will return to resume occupancy if the temple or building is still vacant. Ownership must be proclaimed. Evidence of that ownership must be presented through the title deed or earnest (deposit) given. God's Word, His Holy Spirit, and the godly activity that follows must be evident. I have participated in praying for people to be set free or healed. Once it is evident that they are free or have received healing, we have stressed the need for them to get into the Word of God, to continue being filled with the Spirit, and to stay connected to the Body of Christ. At the time, many agree and follow through, sometimes only for a short period. If they gravitate back to their old lifestyle, they wind up being worse than before. Why? Because when the enemy comes back and they are not filled with the things of God, they are not strong enough to resist the tricks of the devil. Besides that, the demon that got kicked out brings a stronger demon with him to maintain occupancy. People have the right to choose, but we must do our part to make sure they understand the seriousness of remaining unoccupied, decorated, and swept clean. We must let the Word of God occupy every void and leave no room for any of the enemy's tactics to move back into our souls.

Declaration and Confession:

I am thankful for the cleansing power of God. When I am cleansed, I keep myself filled with the Word of God and His precious Holy Spirit. I choose to maintain membership with the Body of Christ. I am free spirit, soul, and body. By the stripes of Jesus, I am healed! I am the redeemed and I say so!

Prayer:

Lord God,

Forgive me for making wrong decisions that have cost me my freedom. You sent Jesus so I would have a way of escape. Thank you for setting me free! Holy Spirit, help me to understand the Word of God, so I can develop into the image of Christ and keep the enemy out. I know that with your help, I can maintain my freedom. Remain strong in me, for Greater is He that is in me than me that is in the world. In Jesus' Mighty Name, Amen.

Reflections:

In what areas do you need the broom of the Holy Spirit to sweep out clutter in your life? Ask Him to do just that, then stay clean and free with the daily reading of God's Word!

Memory Verse: Romans 5:3 – 5 Moreover [let us also be full of joy now!] let us exult and triumph in our troubles and rejoice in our sufferings, knowing that pressure and affliction and hardship produce patient and unswerving endurance. And endurance (fortitude) develops maturity of character (approved faith and tried integrity). And character [of this sort] produces [the habit of] joyful and confident hope of eternal salvation. Such hope never disappoints or deludes or shames us, for God's love has been poured out in our hearts through the Holy Spirit who has been given to us.

Thought of the Day: The Love of God In Us!

---

*H*as God's love on the inside of you been put to the test? My introduction to the baptism in the Holy Spirit brought with it the left foot of fellowship from the pastor of my traditional Baptist church. At the time I was excited about my newfound love for Jesus. The Holy Spirit was overflowing in me and I wanted to share God's love with everyone. I wanted them to know how real God really was. I wanted them to experience the vibrant power of God I was feeling on the inside. Little did I know or understand that my desire to share would be rejected by many people in our faith community. In fact, I was looked upon as the enemy who was spreading propaganda among the members. Because I was a woman and one of the leaders of our women's ministry, the husbands were put on alert to keep me away from their wives. Those who believed the way I did soon left for greener pastures, places of worship where they could freely fellowship and share their spirit-filed experiences without repercussion and retaliation. Although I tried to do the same, the Holy Spirit informed me of my assignment to stay, pray and endure. Sometimes

I felt all alone, but the Spirit of God proved to me that He indeed was the Comforter, Counselor, Helper, Advocate, Intercessor, Strengthener, and Standby. He never left me alone and for that I am so grateful!

During the eight years that followed, the joy of the Lord sustained me even in the midst of persecution. I was silenced when I wanted to speak. I learned to honor the office of the pastor, regardless of my personal beliefs. Even though I was often misunderstood, there were times of triumph and rejoicing. The Holy Spirit used me at poignant times. I learned how to follow the lead of the Holy Spirit and to hear the voice of God. I know for sure that this kind of pressure produces endurance and even when I wanted to give up and move on, I didn't. Although I have a long way to go, I believe I developed maturity of character. My adventure caused my faith to increase. The prayers that the Holy Spirit prayed through me brought the manifestation of hope for a new pastor and spirit-filled experience at the church I was asked to remain in. Today, I am experiencing the results of patient endurance. My faith and integrity have been tried. I'm constantly learning and maturing. I am confident of the eternal salvation I have gained. I (along with my husband) am an ordained minister and leader in the same church that once excluded women from the pulpit and silenced me in particular because of my beliefs in the gifts of the Holy Spirit. After all that I've been through, I am not disappointed and bear no shame. I've learned how to rely on the love of God that resides in my heart through the Holy Spirit. Without that love, I don't know what I would have done. God's Love is true and He's given it to us! If you're experiencing a trial today, I pray this brief testimony will strengthen you and encourage you to rely on the unfailing love of God to sustain you as He matures you, protects you, and victoriously rescues you!

Declaration and Confession:

The Love of God is in my heart! It causes me to endure. Joy has sustained me and caused me to triumph! I am determined to mature. My hope is in the Lord of my salvation. I am not disappointed or ashamed! The Holy Spirit is in me and He does the work!

Prayer:

Dear Lord Jesus,

Thank you for the favor of God that's on my life, because of you! I have learned to endure because of the love that has been placed in my heart. Please help me to mature and develop the faith Your Spirit provides. In you, I am confident that my hopes and dreams will come to pass. I love you, Lord! In Jesus' Mighty Name, Amen.

Reflections:

God's love has been shed abroad in your heart. Rejoice in His agape love and apply it in every situation of your life!

Memory Verse: Philippians 4:17 – 19 Not that I seek or am eager for [your] gift, but I do seek and am eager for the fruit which increases to your credit [the harvest of blessing that is accumulating to your account]. But I have [your full payment] and more; I have everything I need and am amply supplied, now that I have received from Epaphroditus the gifts you sent me. [They are the] fragrant odor of an offering and sacrifice which God welcomes and in which He delights. And my God will liberally supply (fill to the full) your every need according to His riches in glory in Christ Jesus.

Thought for the Day: Your Heavenly Account

We're constantly being told to invest our money in the right place. Many of us are afraid of the stock market and prefer using the bank to save our money in. We try to figure out which stocks or bonds we should invest in. We certainly don't want to be made a fool of. We may even keep it under the mattress or hide it somewhere else in our home. So, we're very cautious about what we do with our money. Never mind the fact that we throw a lot of it away on senseless things, but that's our prerogative, right?

God has a giving system that far surpasses what we have on earth. When it comes to giving in church, we have a whole list of concerns. We certainly don't want to have our money misused by the leadership of our church. Exactly what are they going to do with our offering? Although tithing is being taught as God's way of financing the Kingdom, we need them to give us a report on where the tithes went. We better not see anything out of the ordinary show up, like a new car, nice clothes, or a new home for the first family. Thankfully, many saints have grown passed these concerns and have a great attitude about giving to the church. They know God is a just God and knows how to deal with those who misuse their giving. In today's scripture, Paul is telling these saints that he is grateful for all that they have given to support him. He is also excited about the fruit that their giving has produced for the Kingdom and the interest they are receiving to their heavenly account! He realizes that they have made personal sacrifices to make sure his needs are met. Moreover, he tells them that God is delighted because they have made these sacrificial offerings.

God is aware of the level of sacrifice each one of us makes. It may not be monetary. It may be a sacrifice of time or a decision to give up our desires to line up with His desire for our life. It may be something we do without understanding why He's asking us to do it, but we are obedient, nonetheless. We may stop doing what gives us pleasure to reach out to someone in need. All of these things are contributions of the heart and they bring great dividends! We never fully know how our funding the kingdom will have phenomenal, life-changing effects on people, some of whom we've never even met! Likewise, we cannot even calculate the returns we are getting on our contributions to the kingdom of God. Regardless of how God chooses to bless our benevolence, this scripture tells us we can be sure of this: God liberally supplies our every need! Not according to what or how we invest, but according to His riches in Glory, as we are in Christ Jesus. His only begotten Son has everything His inheritance brings and He's willing to share it with us! He's sharing this inexhaustible wealth while we're here on earth and there will be more when we get home to heaven. And thanks be to God, that even as the old song says, we can't beat God's giving! He blesses us far above our offering to him and loves us far beyond what even our best acts could merit. Our heavenly account is based on God's goodness, if we have a need, make a withdrawal from the heavenly account of God's limitless supply!

Declaration and Confession:

I have a heavenly account! My God supplies every one of my needs. His giving surpasses mine in phenomenal ways. When I have a need, I can withdraw from my heavenly account! I give because of my relationship with God the Father, the Son, and Holy Spirit. It's a blessing to give, yet, I am also blessed to receive what my God has to give!

Prayer:

Dear Father God,

Thank you for supplying ALL of my needs! You give me the means to share what I have with others. It blesses me to give, but I can't out give you. Help me to hear your voice when it comes to giving. I want to plant where you want me to so I can continue to reap a heavenly harvest. When I have a need, I am not worried because You supply my needs! In Jesus' Mighty Name, Amen.

Reflections:

Based on this devotional entry, what are you trusting God for today?

Memory Verse: Proverbs 30:32 If you have done foolishly in exalting yourself, or if you have thought evil, lay your hand upon your mouth.

Thought for the Day: Cover Your Mouth!

*H*ave you ever been so frustrated in a situation or circumstance that you found yourself blurting out a bunch of words that didn't make sound natural or spiritual sense? I must confess that I have, many times, but one incident really sticks out in my mind. My husband and I were going through a financial struggle around Christmas time. All of our sons were grown and gone from our household. They had each finished college and were on their own. Things got so tight that I wasn't going to be able to do what I usually did in buying gifts for those we loved. This really bothered me and I was struggling to keep my mind in the right place. I was on the verge of losing perspective on the fact that "Jesus was the Reason for the Season!"

Mentally, I began to think all sorts of crazy things. We had been blessed most of our marriage to be stable in our finances, even as a young couple. We were able to lend and not borrow. We were able to reach out our hands to our parents and support them physically and emotionally. We had even housed members of our family in our home during hardship or illness until they were able to stand on their own. A parent and grandparent went home to Glory while they were living with us. I was used to being in the "provision" seat. I forgot who allowed us to be able to do all of these things and began to think it was by our might and power. Things got so bad that one of our sons offered to send me some money to do what I needed to do. Now, that really got to me. I said, "We're the parents; we should be sending money to him. I don't like taking money from our children." I was really fussing and complaining about the state we were in. Finally, I spoke these same words to our Co-Pastor and she looked at me and said, "You're just full of pride. That's really what's wrong with you. There's nothing wrong with your adult son extending help to his parents. Didn't you raise them up to be godly men of integrity? What's wrong with him helping his parents in their time of need? Haven't you supported them all of their lives?" Of course, I said yes, but I still thought he shouldn't have to help us. We should be in the position to be supporting them. I hadn't considered that we had been of some sort of assistance to our own parents and grandparents and that life and family are built to be reciprocal. We are all called upon to give - and sometimes, we all will need to gratefully receive. I really couldn't see the blessing in the fact that we had raised sons who were now able and willing to support us! Although I didn't tell her at the time, I was really angry about my pastor's accusation. I was not being proud. I was being a loving parent. I was disappointed to be in the shape we were in. It took a while, but one day I realized that she was right! I had to deal with my pride issue and ask God to forgive me. The pride and all those thoughts in my head had come pouring out of my mouth. I was embarrassed, depressed, anxious, and afraid that we were not going to recover. Pure and simple, I was listening to the enemy! If you do that, he will have you talking foolishly, fill you with pride, and give you evil thoughts. I had to get my heart right, so my mouth would line up with the Word of God. Even now that financial times are better for us, if one of my sons desires to bless me (monetarily or any other way), I gladly receive their offerings. I had to repent and cover all those words with the Blood of Jesus. Please remember to guard your thoughts and trust God! Then, you won't have to Cover Your Mouth!

Declaration and Confession:

I will not exalt myself above my God who is the Provider! The Holy Spirit will help me to keep my thoughts pure. He will shine a light on those things that don't belong, so I can cast them down! Then, I won't have to cover my mouth!

Prayer:

Dear Lord, thank you for forgiving me of my foolish thoughts and cleansing my heart. I will trust you to meet every one of my needs. In Jesus' Mighty Name, Amen.

Reflections:

Think about the things that have come out of your mouth. Were they of God? If not, cover your mouth with faith, not doubt, and you will release life into the atmosphere. The power of life and death are in your tongue!

Memory Verse: Psalms 118:24, 25 This is the day which the Lord has brought about; we will rejoice and be glad in it. Save now, we beseech You, O Lord; send now prosperity, O Lord, we beseech You, and give to us success!

Thought for the Day: Rejoice, This Day!

As I get progressively older, I am convinced that we need to give thanks to the Lord for each day we are privileged to witness. There are those that we don't know and those that we know well and dearly, leaving the planet earth daily. So, when we wake up to a new day, we can say: "This is the day, this is the day, that the Lord has made, that the Lord has made; we will rejoice, we will rejoice and be glad in it!" As the song says, we need to be glad about what God is about to do, today, in our lives. Every moment He gives us to testify of His goodness is a moment to be filled with gratitude. Because He is Jehovah Jireh, Our Provider, we can come to Him boldly as His children and ask Him for prosperity in every area of our lives. We want to prosper in our spirits (where the Holy Spirit resides), in our souls (our mind, will, and emotions), and our bodies (our physical housing). Spiritual prosperity is our top priority, because if we are in alignment with the Spirit of God, he will cause us to prosper in all the other areas of life. We want to have the mind of Christ so we can operate the way He did when He was on the earth. We want our will to submit to the Spirit of God so we can go in the direction God wants us to go in. Therefore, we seek God daily for His divine wisdom and knowledge to make it through each day. If we can keep our emotions in check, we are truly blessed children of God. Our desire is to represent Him well in the earth. We belong to royalty and should walk each day as sons and daughters of the Most High God and heirs to the awesome Kingdom of God! Allowing God to do all that is necessary to bring success into our lives makes each day a day of rejoicing! Then, we can truly say: "This is the day, this is the day; That the Lord has made, that the Lord has made; I will rejoice, I will rejoice; and be glad in it, and be glad in it!" Why don't you REJOICE on this day!

Declaration and Confession:

Today is the day that I will rejoice! I am alive and God has blessed me to see another day! I am glad, because I have another chance to speak of the goodness of God. He has mercy on me and grants me His favor, so I can have success here on earth. I claim prosperity in my spirit, soul, and body. I rejoice, this day!

Prayer:

Dear Father God,

I rejoice in who I am as part of your Kingdom. Thank you for your lovingkindness and tender mercy! You love me unconditionally. So I take each day as a gift from You. Please lead me and guide into the path of success that you have set aside for me. I have much to be thankful for, so I rejoice this day! In the Mighty Name of Jesus, Amen.

Reflections:

Rejoice in the Lord always and again, I say Rejoice!

Memory Verse: Psalms 23:1 – 3 The Lord is my Shepherd [to feed, guide, and shield me]. I shall not lack. He makes me lie down to [fresh, tender] green pastures. He leads me beside the still and restful waters. He refreshes and restores my life (my self); He leads me in the paths of righteousness [uprightness and right standing with Him — not for my earning it, but] for His name's sake.

Thought for the Day: The Lord, My Shepherd!

I read that a secondary definition for sheep is a stupid or timid person. Now, I have heard that sheep are really dumb animals, but this definition called people dumb. What a rude awakening! I know people don't always operate as though we have great intelligence, but I hadn't thought of us as stupid. Our poor pastors have really got their hands full! They are stuck with leading a bunch of sheep! Jesus described Himself as the Good Shepherd who protects the sheep from the thief who comes to steal, kill, and destroy the sheep. If He's the Good Shepherd, there must be some bad shepherds around, too. I believe that the majority of shepherds over the sheep are people who love the Lord and sacrifice their own comforts to watch over the sheep. Every one of them has imperfections and is not perfect, like the Good Shepherd is. However, they are called to study to rightly divide the Word of God so they can feed, guide, and shield the sheep. Some shepherds are misguided or selfish people out to do harm to the sheep for their own purposes. These shepherds come in from somewhere other than through the door of the Good Shepherd. So, as sheep, we had better allow the Holy Spirit in us to distinguish between imperfect shepherds and bad shepherds.

Jesus, the Good Shepherd, always has our best interest at heart. It's His desire that we eat the right food like the (rhema) fresh, revealed Word of God. If we let Him, He will guide us and protect us. He will provide every single one of our needs. As we relax in His presence, He brings peace and rest to our spirit. The oil of His Holy Spirit nourishes our soul. Although the storms of life threaten us, He restores calm to our atmosphere. It gives Him great pleasure to be the connection in our relationship with God the Father. Even in our imperfections, He presents us blameless to His Father. He and the Father welcome us in as vital members of their immediate family. All of the looming anxieties of life that cause us to be fearful are eliminated. His love for us brings us supernatural comfort and peace. There are those that are out to destroy us, but they can't move Him out of the way! He stands tall and strong within us to shield us from their attacks. His goodness, mercy, and overwhelming love surround us. He will never fail or leave us alone. All we have to do is accept Him as our Good Shepherd and all of these benefits become ours. We are no longer sheep without a shepherd. We are no longer stupid, timid, or vulnerable. His house of prayer, joy, love, and peace belong to us. We can dwell there for eternity! I'm so glad that the Lord, the Good Shepherd, is my Shepherd!

Declaration and Confession:

I am a sheep protected by the Good Shepherd! Although I am imperfect, He restores me and gives me right standing with God the Father. Every one of my needs are met by Him. He gives me rest and refreshes me. I can relax in His presence. Thank God! He is the Lord, my Shepherd!

Prayer:

Dear Lord Jesus,

Thank you for being My Shepherd! You shield me from my enemies. You lead, guide and direct me in the paths of health and safety. I come through You to the Father. I love You and appreciate all You do for me. In the Mighty Name of Jesus, I pray, Amen.

Reflections:

Are you wanting for anything? Ask the Lord, Your Shepherd, to supply your needs and you shall not want!

Memory Verse: 2 Kings 5:25 – 27 He went in and stood before his master, Elisha said. Where have you been, Gehazi? He said, Your servant went nowhere. Elisha said to him, Did not my spirit go with you when the man turned from his chariot to meet you? Was it a time to accept money, garments, olive orchards, vineyards, sheep, oxen, menservants, and maidservants? Therefore the leprosy of Naaman shall cleave to you and to your offspring forever. And Gehazi went from his presence a leper as white as snow.

Thought for the Day: A High Price to Pay for Greed!

This is a very sad story about the results of envy and greed. Gehazi had been a loyal servant to the Prophet Elisha. He had seen God use Elisha to do mighty exploits. He had been the messenger and armor bearer for Elisha. How did he manage to listen to the devil and find himself in such a predicament? Any of us can allow the voice of the enemy to override the voice of God at any given time. Therefore, we must take heed to this lesson suffered by Gehazi. It's bad enough to be guilty of lying, being envious of another's position, and being greedy. It's worse to have been in the presence of God at work and still not maintain a pure heart towards God and His leaders.

In this story, Naaman had previously come to Elisha for healing of leprosy. He was insulted, because he was a commander of the army of the King of Syria and considered to be a mighty man of valor, yet, Elisha had sent word by his servant and didn't even bother to come out in person. Elisha wanted Naaman to dip 7 times in the Jordan River to be relieved of his leprosy. Naaman was furious, because Elisha had not shown him proper respect and was asking him to dip in the filthy Jordan River. His servants encouraged him to go ahead and obey the request of the prophet. He was wise enough to do so and was completely healed! He learned a valuable lesson about pride that had almost cost him his healing. As a result he wanted to reward the prophet. Elisha turned down his offer of payment and was satisfied with Naaman's change of heart towards God. His servant Gehazi overheard the offer made to Elisha and decided to receive the reward for himself. He forfeited his integrity with God and position with the man of God. He listened to the temptation of the enemy to lie, and he became envious and greedy for material gain. He thought, "if Elisha won't receive this reward, I will." He didn't realize how God felt about this deceit and greed. It was evil in the sight of God. He forgot that God was his provider, even after watching Him provide over and over again for his master. And if God had made provision for his master, he had also made provision for Gehazi time and time again. This moment of greed not only cost him, but his generations were also doomed forever. No matter what our position is in the Kingdom of God, He knows what's in our heart. And as it was in this case, our heart often dictates our actions. Gehazi paid a very high price for this display of greed. We must remain on guard, not simply to do what is right, but to keep our hearts in the right place. Greed can slap us in the face with a bill that's too costly to pay!

Declaration and Confession:

I will open my heart to God and his leaders. I will not allow envy and greed to override what I know about God's ability to provide for me. I will take what God is doing around me, for me, and through me seriously and listen to those with whom I have accountability. Because of the Spirit of God in me, I will be content and trust God to remain my Provider.

Gwendolyn F. Mosley

Prayer:

Dear Lord Jesus,

Help me to be content where I am, because I know that you love me and God will provide my every need. My desire is to be used by you to benefit the Kingdom of God. The Greater One in me will cancel the temptations of the enemy that come my way as I submit to Him. In Jesus' Name, Amen.

Reflections:

Examine your heart and make sure that there is no deceit hidden there. Trust God to provide the desires of your heart.

Memory Verse: Psalm 62:1, 2 For God alone my soul waits in silence; from Him comes my Salvation. He only is my Rock and my Salvation, my Defense and my Fortress. I shall not be greatly moved.

Thought for the Day: My Rock, Salvation, Defense, and Fortress!

Woe to those who choose to mess with us! God is our Rock! Upon this Rock, I will build my church, and the gates of hell shall not prevail against it! What Rock is this? It's the revelation of who Jesus is! He is the only begotten Son of God! The one God sent to be our Salvation! Jesus, the eternal Lamb of God who took away the sins of the world! His blood was shed to cover a multitude of our sins. We never have to sacrifice another lamb, dove, ram, or anything else. His blood is the sufficient sacrifice for us. He has saved us from ALL destruction! Jesus is our Defense! We were guilty of sin or treason against God, but Jesus stands in our defense against every accusation of the enemy. What He did on the cross took away the penalty of the eternal death we were due. We now have right standing with God the Father, because of what Jesus has done for us. He is our protection against the wrath of God. Jesus is our Fortress! We are in a fortified place by the power of His Blood. Our position with God is secure!

Because of all that Jesus has done for us, no matter what our soul is confronted with, we should not be greatly moved. We should not be moved into panic by the thoughts that enter our mind, the emotions we feel on the inside, and we should not be controlled by our own wills. If we will close our mouths and allow the Spirit of God to rule and reign in our situations, we will come out on top - standing tall on top of the Rock of our Salvation, Jesus! If we will listen to the Spirit of God on the inside of us, we will speak the words that will come to our defense in any circumstance. The Fortress God has set around our heart through Jesus causes us to stand still and depend on God. Therefore, we will not be moved by what's going on around us. Our concern will turn into trust, so we are not greatly moved! We will not lean to our own understanding, but we will acknowledge the God of Our Salvation and know we are safe! He is our Rock, Salvation, Defense, and Fortress. So, In Him will be trust!

Declaration and Confession:

In the midst of my concerns and trouble, I know that God is My Rock, Salvation, Defense, and Fortress! I may find myself under attack, but God has made a way of escape for me. I will close my mouth and listen to my heart so I will speak the words that bring deliverance my way. I am not moved by what I see. I walk by faith and not by sight!

Prayer:

Father God,

Thank you for rescuing me from All of my distress! I can depend on you to deliver me from all of my fears. As I lean and depend on You, I get the courage to stand still and see your salvation. Because of Your Spirit in me, I will walk by faith and maintain Your sight. Your perfect will be done in my life! In Jesus' Mighty Name, Amen.

Gwendolyn F. Mosley

Reflections:

When did you last feel a little stressed out? What did you do to alleviate that stress? After reading this entry, I hope you know to overcome stress, trust in God the Rock of your salvation!

Memory Verse: 2 Kings 6:15 – 17 When the servant of the man of God rose early and went out, behold, an army with horses and chariots was around the city. Elisha's servant said to him, Alas, my master! What shall we do? [Elisha] answered, Fear not; for those with us are more than those with them. Then Elisha prayed, Lord, I pray You, open his eyes that he may see. And the Lord opened the young man's eyes and he saw, and behold, the mountain was full of horses and chariots of fire round about Elisha.

Thought for the Day: There Are More With Us!

Have you ever been in a threatening position and outnumbered? Have you ever asked for God's assistance in a life-threatening situation? Do you believe that God loves you and will send you the support you need in times of peril? Sometimes we find ourselves in these positions of discomfort or threat and we pray and ask for God's help, but do we really believe that He hears us and answers our prayers? Sometimes we believe God can, but do we believe that God will do what is needed for us, personally?

This scripture reminds me of the time my dad was critically ill. My sister-in-law and I went into the room he had been assigned to and prayed over the intensive care unit he was in. During our prayer, we asked God for the protection of His angels to watch over him. We left there confident that God had heard our prayer, but not really assured of the importance of our request to God. We really wanted God to protect my dad, yet, we didn't really think He was taking our request literally. Several days later, my brother (who had no idea what we had prayed) came to visit my dad. He said, when he walked into the room there were angels posted on each side of our dad's bed. He said they were 9 to 10 feet tall and could describe what they were wearing in detail. Although he felt a little startled, he knew immediately that they were angels. So, he moved in closer and blinked to make sure he was really seeing what he thought he was seeing. The angels were still there! Then, he decided he would look at their faces to see if he could recognize them. When he did this, their faces looked wavy, as if they were under water and he could not determine any distinct features. He talked to my dad, who was in a coma, briefly and carefully backed out of the room. Later that day, he informed us of his encounter with the angels. To our amazement, God had answered our prayer, literally! God hears our prayers and will do exactly what we request when our request is scripturally supported. At the time, I was not aware of the significance of this scripture. However, God proved that He is concerned about His servants and protects us in our time of need. So if you ever feel threatened, outnumbered, or in a time of peril call on God for reinforcements and know in your spirit that there are more with us than with our enemies or enemy!

Declaration and Confession:

I believe God hears my prayers! I know He loves me and is interested in my safety and protection. When I am in trouble of any sort, He cares about me! The enemy may send a host against me, but the army of God is greater! He sends His angels on my behalf (Psalm 34:7), so I can depend on my God!

Prayer:

Dear Lord Jesus,

You are King of Kings and Lord of Lords! You hear me when I pray. You sit at the right hand of God, ever interceding for me. I can call on God the Father to send His angels to protect me. I have guardian angels who watch over me! I need not fear for God is always with me! In Jesus' Mighty Name, Amen.

Reflections:

Have you ever been in a situation or circumstance that caused your heart to tremble? How did God show up on your behalf?

Memory Verse: 1 Corinthians 3:16, 17 Do you not discern and understand that you [the whole church at Corinth] are God's temple (His sanctuary), and that God's Spirit has His permanent dwelling in you [to be at home in you, collectively as a church and also individually]? If anyone does hurt to God's temple or corrupts it [with false doctrines] or destroys it, God will do hurt to him and bring him to the corruption of death and destroy him. For the temple of God is holy (sacred to Him) and that [temple] you [the Believing church and its individual believers] are.

Thought for Today: What Makes Us Holy?

Just think, the Holy Spirit of the living God, lives on the inside of us! Every time I think about that, I just marvel at the love of God for us that would cause Him to choose us to make His home in. Where we live is an important part of how we feel about going home. I'll always remember the response from my middle son, Donavan, one day at the age of 16. He walked through the door of our house after school one day, sprawled himself on the den floor, and said; "I'm so glad to be home!" That moment has never faded from my mind, because I was so pleased to see that a 16-year-old young man could be that relaxed and at peace in his home while other boys his age were anxious to see what the world outside of their homes had to offer. That's how the Holy Spirit wants to feel inside of us. He wants to live in someone who loves God, relishes His presence, and shows that love to other people. God is not into our religious rituals. He's about us having a life of abundance in love, joy, and peace. No one wants to go to a house full of chaos, anger, hate, fear, corruption, and lawlessness. Those attributes do not make a secure home. There are neighborhoods in every city that are on that unofficial list of places to stay away from because of the violence they represent. Authorities tell you quickly to stay away from that part of town. When we are about to purchase a home, we look for a quiet neighborhood with beautiful homes. They may not be huge homes, but they are a nice size and in a peaceful place.

God is looking to live inside of those who welcome him and have a desire to be like Him. He wants offspring that resemble Him in their actions. He wants them to be people who live in the world to make it better. He wants them to be interested in the needs of others because He's all about meeting needs. He wants them to be willing to submit to His Holy Spirit, so they can become powerful in disbursing darkness. The light that the Holy Spirit brings will shine through them to rescue a dying world. That's why He sent Jesus in the first place to eliminate the darkness of the world. As they allow the Holy Spirit to override their natural tendencies, He will lead them into the presence of Jesus. In turn, they will have an encounter with the loving Father. It's the Father in them that makes them Holy. This is really how we want to live and where the Spirit of God wants to live. God wants to live comfortably in us, as my son lived in our home. So, what really makes us holy? It's not about being at church every Sunday, even though Believers should want to associate with and support each other. We should want to come together and worship and praise our Holy God. Going to church is like going to a family reunion, so we should want to attend. However, it's really about being sons and daughters of a Holy God. He is a Holy God and His DNA in us makes us Holy!

Declaration and Confession:

I am holy because God is holy! I belong to Him and have His DNA. So, it's my desire to meet the needs of other people. It's not just about me and my three. The peace of God in me makes me comfortable in my own skin. I am busy seeking God's nature and quality of life!

Prayer:

Dear Father God,

Thank You for choosing to live in me by Your Spirit. Help me to represent You in the earth. Because I belong to You, I will allow Your light to shine through me. Jesus, in me, sets me free! In Jesus' Mighty Name, Amen.

Reflections:

You are a spirit, you have a soul, and live in a body. What kind of house do you live in?

Memory Verse: 2 Corinthians 1:18 – 20 As surely as God is trustworthy and faithful and means what He says, our speech and message to you have not been Yes [that might mean] No. For the Son of God, Christ Jesus (the Messiah), Who has been preached among you by us, by myself, Silvanus, and Timothy, was not Yes and No, but in Him it is [always the divine] Yes. For as many as are the promises of God, they all find their Yes [answer] in Him [Christ]. For this reason we also utter the Amen (so be it) to God through Him [in His Person and by His agency] to the glory of God.

Thought for the Day! Yes and Amen!

---

*H*ave you ever made a promise that you were unable to keep? Most of the time, I believe people make promises based on what they think they can do. However, things happen that we cannot foresee that cause us to disappoint others because we fail to come through on a promise we made. That's why I tried not to make too many promises to my sons when they were growing up. Not being able to keep a promise to a child can be devastating for them, depending on what the promise is. As they get older, they become aware of life's challenges and are not as easily hurt or disappointed for occasional broken promises. Anyone would become irritated by constant breaking of promises from someone they believe in and care about. The trust and strength of such a relationship would soon dissolve from this kind of reckless behavior. In this day and time, a person keeping their word in our society has become a lost art, so our expectations in the business and political arena are not very high.

Our scripture today is reminding us of the certainty of God's Word. When He makes a promise to us, we can be sure that He will come through. He is not a man that He should lie or a parent that won't keep His promise to His child. He is a faithful and trustworthy God, so His Yes means Yes. Because God knows the beginning, middle, and the end; His Yes is a divine guarantee. Jesus told the disciples that His temple would be destroyed and be back in three days. That's exactly what happened! He said He would send the Comforter (the Holy Spirit), because He was leaving to go to His Father. That's exactly what happened! He said, He would never leave us or forsake us in the time of trouble. That's exactly what happens when we are in distress and peril, but we have to be aware of His faithfulness in the midst of life's storms. He will speak "peace be still" to the winds and waves of our storms if we believe He is there to come to our rescue. Sometimes we are not aware at the time of trouble, but later on, we see that He was there all the time. We discover that He had carried us to safety in His loving arms. Our ultimate promise is: absent from the body, present with the Lord! That is our expectation and belief, because God has come through for us on so many occasions that we have no reason to doubt this promise. So, to the Glory of Almighty God, based on His Son, Jesus Christ, we take every one of His promises to mean: Yes and Amen (so be it)!

Declaration and Confession:

I believe the promises of God! When a promise is made in the Word of God, I know that the answer is, Yes and Amen! My times of trouble prove to be an opportunity for God to show Himself strong in my life. So, I have confidence in the God I serve, because of the promises kept through His Son Jesus!

Prayer:

Dear Lord Jesus,

Thank you for the many promises you've made and kept! My faith and trust in You is strong. I know you are not a man that You would lie to me. Your Word is true! So, to God Be the Glory for the things He has done and will do in my life. In the Name of Jesus, Yes and Amen (so be it).

Reflections:

God is NOT a man that He would lie. Trust Him to keep His promises today and always.

Memory Verse: Matthew 27:51 – 53 And at once the curtain of the sanctuary of the temple was torn in two from top to bottom; the earth shook and the rocks were split. The tombs were opened and many bodies of the saints who had fallen asleep in death were raised [to life]; And coming out of the tombs after His resurrection, they went into the holy city and appeared to many people.

Thought for the Day: A Surprise Visit!

This is a very interesting passage of scripture. Yet, I've never heard a portion of it preached. When Jesus died on the cross (giving up His spirit), some amazing things happened in an instant. The veil tore from top to bottom, signifying the end of our separation from God, meaning we are now able to go directly to God for ourselves. Jesus was now the High Priest who presented His blood to the Father on our behalf once for eternity. No more sacrifices were needed. The earth shook violently, causing rocks to split, and an earthquake occurred. God was making His presence known in all of these occurrences.

Another surprising event was the opening of the tombs! The scripture says many bodies of the saints who had died were raised to life. We're always talking about the return of Jesus Christ, when the dead in Christ will rise. This tells us that has already happened once. Not only did they rise, they went into the holy city and appeared to many people. Yet, there is no story recorded in the Bible by someone who received one of these surprise visits. This incident alone should have been the talk of the city. In fact, the centurion and those with him were extremely frightened and in total awe of these acts of God. So I guess there wasn't anyone brave enough to report any visits. After all, those who had killed Jesus were still alive and well. They were ready to kill anyone who dared to identify themselves with this Jesus. He was the troublemaker who was a vagabond imposter claiming to rise after three days. They did everything they could to keep this from happening. They secured the tomb with a sealed boulder. Then, they stationed guards around it to make sure no one was able to come and steal His body by the third day. It would be utter chaos for His disciples to be able to proclaim that He had risen from the grave as He had said.

If you were living during this time, what would you have done? Suppose one of those saints from the grave yard had come knocking at your door. Even if it was a loved one that you were thrilled to see, would you have been brave enough to tell others about your visitor? These were extraordinary, strange happenings and most people would have thought you had lost your mind! Only those who were believers of Jesus Christ would even dare to believe such a story. The mere fact that we believe that Jesus, the Son of God, came to this earth, did many wonders, was crucified, died, and rose again is unbelievable to those who don't believe. I believe that Jesus Christ is coming back to receive us and the dead in Christ will rise again, just as they did in this passage. So, it's not hard for me to believe that there were many at this time who received A Surprise Visit! I dare you to believe in the extraordinary. God is used to showing out - doing the seemingly impossible. Be ready for a surprise visit of this magnitude! God can bless you out of, in the midst of, and through any dying situation. He can revive your hope and your heart. 'Only believe! We must be ready for A Surprise Visit!

Declaration and Confession:

I believe the unbelievable! Jesus Christ, the Messiah, gave His life to rescue me! He kept His word and rose on the third day to present His blood as the Holy Sacrifice for my sins and the sins of the world to His Father. I want to be ready when He comes again. So, I must work the works of Him who sent me, while it is day for when night comes no man will work. I believe that God is authorizing A Surprise Visit just for me!

Prayer:

Lord Jesus,

Thank you for coming to redeem me! Help me to be brave enough to proclaim you to those who don't believe. I need the Holy Spirit to lead, guide, and direct me into all truth. Your Word is truth and I know that it sets me free. In the Mighty Name of Jesus, I pray, Amen.

Reflections:

Do you believe in the resurrected Christ? I pray you do, but if not, now's the time to believe and accept His resurrected life for yourself. Then, you too can have expectant faith to believe the impossible!

Memory Verse: 2 Corinthians 4:16 – 18 Therefore we do not become discouraged (utterly spiritless, exhausted, and wearied out through fear). Though our outer man is [progressively] decaying and wasting away, yet our inner self is being [progressively] renewed day after day. For our light, momentary affliction (this slight distress of the passing hour) is ever more and more abundantly preparing and producing and achieving for us an everlasting weight of glory [beyond all measure, excessively surpassing all comparisons and all calculations, a vast and transcendent glory and blessedness never to cease!] Since we consider and look not to the things that are seen but to the things that are unseen; for the things that are visible are temporal (brief and fleeting), but the things that are invisible are deathless and everlasting.

Thought For the Day: Don't Look!

You may be going through something right now; sickness, unemployment, loss of a loved one, disappointment, financial struggles, some form of addiction, or depression, to name a few. While you're in the midst of hard times, it is easy to become discouraged. When we become discouraged, our reservoir of joy is depleted. Because the joy of the Lord gives us strength, we lose our energy, our internal fortitude, and we become weak. This weakness causes us to be overcome with exhaustion. The fear of never coming out of this pattern brings hopelessness our way. As children of God, there shouldn't be any reason for us to get into depths of despair, but we allow ourselves to. Although our physical being is moving in the direction of continuous decay, our spirit being is growing stronger each day based on our choice to let the Spirit of God rule and reign in our life. If we don't allow Him to renew us daily, we will feel the effects of what we go through from living in this world.

The truth is the things that we go through are temporary situations and circumstances. However, the lies of the enemy start running through our mind and if we don't throw them out and replace them with the Word of God, it seems like they will never pass, and I believe that it's this very thinking that sometimes prolongs life's trials. But the more we rely on God during these times of distress the more we learn about how the enemy works and the lies he tells. As we gain knowledge and wisdom on how God works, our confidence in what we don't see blocks out what we do see. We cannot allow ourselves to focus on what we are seeing, because our eternal victory comes from our God who we can't see. His existence, power, and authority are more real than the obstacles we are looking at. So, when we're facing something that has the capabilities to take our very life, we have to depend on and totally trust the God we serve. His Spirit is on the inside of us and He is deathless. He is the God of life! He is the Giver and Sustainer of life! There is no death in Him! He is the everlasting God! Anything representing death and destruction comes from the evil one. Jesus came here to give us life in abundance! Our job is to fix our mind on the things that bring life and do them. We are to speak the things that deliver life, as the end result. The enemy comes to steal, kill, and destroy us. So, if what we're looking at is stealing from us, killing us, or destroying us, we simply Don't Look!

Declaration and Confession:

I am not moved by what I see! What I don't see is more real than what I do see! I put my trust in the invisible God I serve. He has all power and authority over my life, if I give it to Him. No distress or affliction has more power than My God! I must trust and believe in Him. Faith is My Master Key to Victory!

Prayer:

Dear Father God,

You know my beginning, middle, and end. I trust you with my life. Your Spirit brings confidence in You, so I can withstand the trials of this life. God, please forgive me for not trusting you and allowing distress to enter into any of my situations or circumstances. I release what I see to You, so what I don't see will come to pass. In Jesus' Mighty Name, Amen.

Reflections:

Sometimes we just need to close our eyes and believe God! How about you, are you walking by faith or by sight?

Memory Verse: Genesis 2:16, 17; 3:1-4 And the Lord God commanded the man, saying, You may freely eat of every tree of the garden. But of the tree of the knowledge of good and evil and blessing and calamity you shall not eat, for in the day that you eat of it you shall surely die. Now the serpent was more subtle and crafty than any living creature of the field which the Lord God had made. And he [Satan] said to the woman. Can it really be that God has said, You shall not eat from every tree of the garden? And the woman said to the serpent. We may eat the fruit from the trees of the garden. Except the fruit from the tree which is in the middle of the garden. God has said, You shall not eat of it, neither shall you touch it, lest you die. But the serpent said to the woman. You shall not surely die.

Thought for the Day:
Deception Breeds Doubt!

Have you ever been given divine instruction from God, been excited, at peace with it, and willing to do it? What usually happens after that? In my experience, something or someone will come right behind that instruction to point out the ifs, ands, or buts. I hear things like, "you didn't really hear from God" or "that doesn't make any sense." These deceptive statements immediately bring doubt into the picture. I start wondering, "did I really hear from God?" A minute ago I was excited and ready to get busy doing what I was told. Following that voice of direction from God could have given me peace in the midst of a storm. Even if I have already tested the spirit by the spirit (1 John 4:1-4), which we should do to make sure we are listening to God, entertaining doubtful statements cause me to second guess what I heard. Hearing that it doesn't make sense causes me to rely on my intellect for confirmation.

My natural mind or intellect cannot understand the things of God, so I am using the wrong tool to judge with. It doesn't have to make sense, because walking by faith does not require details, and God's thoughts are higher than ours (Isaiah 55:8).

The enemy [Satan] made deceptive statements to Eve. She received them and that got this whole ball rolling. He pretends he's trying to verify what God has said. Is it really true that God said you can't eat from every tree of the garden? This is really opposite of what God has said. So when Eve cleared up that deception and points out which tree God has tabooed, he refuted the consequence given by God for violating this command. He said straight out, "you will not surely die." Here, the father of lies is calling God a liar! Each time, he is in direct opposition to God. He has mental keenness and knows how to make fine distinctions on what God has said. We call that splitting hairs. He takes the truth and starts cutting it with strips of deception. This same kind of thinking got him kicked out of heaven. So, being skillful in deception, he gets Eve to start questioning what God has said. After defying the penalty for disobeying God, he begins to point out why God is trying to take advantage of His prize creation. The important takeaway of these scriptures is the fact that we are still being challenged with these deceptive statements. Anytime we are given a directive from God, we are confronted by the same kind of questions. We must learn the lesson from these scriptures and realize how God operates and how Satan operates. No matter how cunning or clever he is in deception and lies, God is more skillful, powerful, and constant in truth. Although it seems like he is not easily detected at times, if we will start being attentive to the Word of God, we will begin to see the differences in what is said and how it is said. This will cause our spiritual ears to be keen in knowing who we are listening to. Also, if we stop questioning everything that God tells us to do and show our trust in Him by doing what He says, we will discover that He loves us and is not out to trip us up or deceive us in any way. His desire is to protect us and give us great success. He wants us to operate by faith and confidence of who He is and not fear of Him doing something detrimental to us. He wants us to know Him so well, that we will recognize those statements of deception and realize that they only bring doubt. Doubt cancels our faith and without faith it is impossible to please God. He wants to reward us for diligently seeking Him! Guard yourself against deception!

Declaration and Confession:

I refuse to listen to the voice of the enemy. The Holy Spirit shines a light on his lies. I will receive the instructions given by God and will obey them. No longer will I allow deception to breed doubt in me!

Prayer:

Dear Father God,

Help me to be discerning in what I hear. Help me to be mindful about whose voice I allow to penetrate my spirit. I love you and want to obey you alone. In Jesus' Name, Amen.

Reflections:

Satan is the great deceiver. Refuse to listen to him, starve your doubt and feed your faith instead!

Memory Verse: 1 Corinthians 2:14 But the natural, nonspiritual man does not accept or welcome or admit into his heart the gifts and teachings and revelations of the Spirit of God, for they are folly (meaningless non-sense) to him; and he is incapable of knowing them [of progressively recognizing, understanding, and becoming better acquainted with them] because they are spiritually discerned and estimated and appreciated.

Thought for the Day: God's Gift of Love

---

*A*s I write this entry, today happens to be the day recognized by many as Valentine's Day. It is a day designated to give honor to those you hold near and dear to your heart. The love industry benefits, as millions of people buy cards, flowers, candy, and other items that signify our love for our spouse, mate, family member, co-workers, friends, students, or classmates. It's an opportunity to express our deep affection for one another or a time to let another person know you like them. It can be very deep love or just a casual acknowledgement of a relationship. God is Love and we were made in His image, so most human beings respond to love that is shown to them by others. It's a good excuse to have a party or enjoy the company of the one you love.

The things we do in the natural on Valentine's Day are things that don't require any spiritual discernment. This verse tells us that God has given us a gift of love that must be received supernaturally. To show His affection for us, He has given us the Holy Spirit. In order to appreciate this gift, we must acknowledge and understand the divine favor and blessing God has lavishly placed upon us. The only way to be able to do that is to have the Holy Spirit deposited in us, when we receive the finished work of Jesus done at the cross. God has freely given us His truth in words that must be interpreted by the Spirit of God. These truths are nonsense to the understanding of the natural man. However, these teachings and revelations are accepted, welcomed, and admitted into the hearts of those who love God and are called according to His purpose for their lives. Just as we choose to love certain people and call them our sweetheart, we have to choose to accept God into our heart. He created us and gave us our very lives, but we must choose to benefit from the gifts our creator has put aside just for us. He will not force us to receive these gifts anymore than it would be beneficial to force your love on someone who doesn't want to receive it. He wants us to accept His love freely. Any relationship requires commitment and responsibility to be maintained. So, in the natural we go out and purchase something to represent our love to those we care about on these designated days. Hopefully, our love is shown daily, but it's still fun to participate on special days. If you haven't accepted this gift of love from God, I recommend that you do. The benefits of a relationship with Him outweigh our natural benefits from other human beings. We do our best to show our love for one another, but no one can beat God with the gifts He gives. His gifts cannot be bought with money. It might seem nice if we could purchase peace, love, and joy. But what a blessing to know that they're free! These gifts can be received from God supernaturally. Take time to receive Him into your heart and enjoy a gift that will last throughout eternity. It's God's gift of Love!

Declaration and Confession:

I choose to accept God's Gift of Love! He gives me a pure love that no man can give. His Holy Spirit reveals His will for my life. The Truth that He brings my way gives me understanding beyond my abilities. I freely receive His peace, love, and joy that sustains me through every situation and circumstance.

Prayer:

Dear Lord God,

Thank you for your undying love. No one can love me like you do. Your love is unconditional. It brings Your peace and joy with it. The Holy Spirit is welcomed to reveal Your truths to me. I want to know You better. I receive the blessings and divine favor you have for me. In Jesus' Mighty Name, Amen.

Reflections:

Even as a Believer, we must continually choose to receive God's gift of Love. Consciously make the choice to accept God's gift today. It's better than a Valentine's Day present!

Memory Verse: 1 Thessalonians 5:15 – 18 See that none of you repays another with evil for evil, but always aim to show kindness and seek to do good to one another and to everybody. Be happy [in your faith] and rejoice and be glad-hearted continually (always); Be unceasing in prayer [praying perseveringly]; Thank [God] in everything [no matter what the circumstances may be, be thankful and give thanks], for this is the will of God for you [who are] in Christ Jesus [the Revealer and Mediator of that will].

Thought for the Day: Don't Stop Praying!

The directives given in this passage of scripture have prayer right in the middle. It is very tempting to return evil to those who have mistreated you. Your flesh would just be so happy and content to reward a nasty deed with one just as bad or worse. That's why we love watching television stories that give the villain of the story their just due. We root for the underdog, because we want people we can relate to, to experience victory. It makes us feel better to know that there is justice given to those who live to crush others. After all, they deserve to be hammered for what they've done, right? The problem with our natural thinking is that we don't want judgment rendered on us when we've done something we should not have done. We want to throw ourselves on the mercy of the court, right?

Next in the text, there's the problem of being thankful in every situation and circumstance we find ourselves in. Sometimes it would just be easier to have a pity party and invite all of our friends to come and moan with us. Why should we be thankful for the things that don't make us feel good? Why do we have to swallow our pride and admit that we are wrong or admit that we have believed a lie? Why do bad things happen to good people? Why do we have to be kind to others and rejoice in the midst of our pain? These questions can only be answered as we seek God in prayer. We are able to rejoice and be glad in our heart during these times, when we have spent time listening to what God is saying about what we are dealing with. Jesus paved the way for us to go to the Father directly to receive help. God knows all about us and will give clear direction during these difficult times because Jesus is our High Priest who goes to Him on our behalf and helps us to carry out the will of our Father. He sent the Comforter (the Holy Spirit) to bring to our memory the things that are in the Word of God that will reveal the victory in every situation. Sometimes, the biggest victory is the change in our attitude and perspective brought about by the faith that we have in who God is and who we are in Him. We learn that we don't have to stoop to the natural way of doing things; we can overcome by operating in love and kindness as prescribed in the Word of God. Forgiveness can be an automatic response, if we practice forgiveness on a regular basis. We can rest in knowing that no matter what we are going through, God has our back! The only way we can be successful in applying this Word is to be persistent in prayer. In other words, don't stop praying!

Declaration and Confession:

I override my flesh with the Word of God! I forgive others no matter how I feel about what they've done to me. I won't return kindness for evil, because the Spirit of God lives inside of me. All things do work together for my good, because God has my back! I pray without stopping!

Prayer:

Dear Lord God,

Things don't always seem fair that happen in my life, but you didn't say they would be. You promised never to leave me or forsake me in the time of trouble. So I depend on you to bring me the victory in every circumstance. Your Spirit gives me the ability to forgive those who mistreat me. Thank You for the privilege of communicating with You in prayer! In Jesus' Mighty Name, Amen.

Reflections:

Is there anything in your life that's begging you to repay a trespasser? Don't do it! Take it to God in prayer, leave it there, and do what He says for you to do.

Memory Verse: Luke 17:11 – 15 As He went on His way to Jerusalem, it occurred that [Jesus] was passing [along the border] between Samaria and Galilee. And as He was going into one village, He was met by ten lepers, who stood at a distance. And they raised up their voices and called, Jesus, Master, take pity and have mercy on us! And when He saw them, He said to them, Go [at once] and show yourselves to the priests. And as they went, they were cured and made clean. Then one of them, upon seeing that he was cured, turned back, recognizing and thanking and praising God with a loud voice.

Thought for the Day: Moving Faith

---

*T*his story inspires me to activate my faith to the extent that, if the Spirit of God tells me to do something, I will do it without hesitation. These ten lepers had evidently heard about Jesus and had enough faith to cry out to Him from a distance. They asked Him to have pity on them and grant them mercy in their serious medical condition. Being full of compassion, Jesus responded to their request by healing them. He did not walk over to them and lay hands on them. He simply spoke a statement of healing to them. They in turn responded by doing what He said with no immediate manifestation. However, as they were obedient, healing manifested in their physical bodies.

How many times has your request for a need been abandoned, because you did not see immediate results? Sadly, I will have to say that this has happened many times in my life. Although I'm getting better at responding without apparent results, it has been a long time coming. God's reputation in the scriptures, the testimonies of others, and particularly in my own life have all proven Him to be a God of His

Word. Yet, I sometimes have the audacity to doubt His ability to back up what He says. I don't know about you, but I want to be like these lepers who obeyed Jesus without seeing immediate results. Even though they were in a position of desperation, they could have rejected His Words and given up hope. They chose to believe what He said and continue on their journey with expectation of a positive result.

Another lesson we can learn from this story is that human beings are generally ungrateful by nature. You would have thought that all ten lepers would have made it back to Jesus to say thanks. They had a death sentence, as well as isolation to contend with. Yet, they did not take the time to show their appreciation. They were outcasts who had to cry out "unclean" as others approached them. To be set free from that kind of aggravation should have caused them to dance, shout, and run to Jesus with gratitude. The sad thing is we are often guilty of the same behavior. No matter how great or how small our need may be, we should always make our requests known to God and then be sure to thank Him when He answers our cry for help. Remember, when you're faced with a dilemma, cry out to God because He will show compassion and mercy. And when he does, be sure you respond with Moving Faith and Thanksgiving!

Declaration and Confession:

I have the kind of faith that moves mountains! When there is a concern in my life, I go to God in prayer and believe I receive the answer to my request. Even if I don't see immediate results, I will be obedient to what the Spirit of God tells me to do. Now faith requires Now action! I have Moving Faith!

Prayer:

Dear Lord Jesus,

Thank you for having compassion that moves You into action! Forgive me for past responses to You that prevented me from receiving what you had for me. I choose to believe the Words You say. I know faith without works is dead. Help me to be obedient to what You say. In Jesus' Mighty Name, Amen.

Reflections:

Are you walking in expectant faith? Trust God and keep moving toward your Victory!

Memory Verse: 1 Thessalonians 4:9 – 11 But concerning brotherly love [for all other Christians], you have no need to have anyone write you, for you yourselves have been [personally] taught by God to love one another. And indeed you already are [extending and displaying your love] to all the brethren throughout Macedonia. But we beseech and earnestly exhort you, brethren, that you excel [in this matter] more and more. To make it your ambition and definitely endeavor to live quietly and peacefully, to mind your own affairs, and to work with your hands, as we charged you.

Thought for the Day: Mind Your Own Biz!

I tell you the truth when I say it takes 24/7 concentration on what I'm doing, thinking, and saying to stay straight! Keeping yourself in check is a lot of work! If we would spend the majority of our time doing that and the remainder of our time loving one another, this world would be a much better place. Actually, I'm just talking about the Body of Christ. The love of God has been deposited in our hearts through the power of the Holy Spirit that is in us. We have the ability to love unconditionally but it takes constant pushing back and rebuking of our natural tendencies for the love in us to stay at the forefront and flow out. The more we practice loving one another, the easier it becomes.

Making this one of our top priorities is needed if we are to live in harmony with mankind. All of us have our little quirks that bother other people. Keeping that in mind, we must be willing to discount the manifestation of other people's annoying habits that trigger a negative response from us. Let's start working at being quiet and peaceful wherever we go. Why not spend time staying in our own lane and allow others to maintain theirs? When we're driving, it is extremely important that we maintain the pathway we are in and signal when we're about to switch lanes to keep from having a collision. If we would do the same thing in our interactions with one another, there would be fewer crashes of our emotions. When it becomes necessary to change lanes, we need to conference with one another and get a clear understanding about the switch we're about to make. Sometimes, just a simple explanation would keep us from stepping on each other's toes. Collaboration is needed and necessary to keep things going in the right direction. There's plenty of work to be done in the Body of Christ, so if we would endeavor to do the work that's been assigned to us by God and our ministry leaders, we just might get a lot done. It would be so nice for the natural world to see us loving on each other and blessing others. They might even come to us for help because they can see we know how to live a godly life. The Spirit of God would be flowing to the extent that the power of God would let them know that we have the answer to life's struggles, sickness, and pain. To be honest, it really isn't as hard as it seems. We simply need to endeavor to Mind Our Own Business!

Declaration and Confession:

Because I want to be a blessing to my fellow man, I have decided that I will spend the time necessary to keep my own life in check. Because of the Holy Spirit in me, I will love others unconditionally as God loves me. I have a lot of work to do, so I will keep myself busy doing what God has called me to do. To do that successfully, I must mind my own business!

Prayer:

Dear Lord Jesus,

You loved me so much that you were willing to die for my sins. I want to have that kind of love for others. Help me by your Spirit to forgive and extend

Gwendolyn F. Mosley

myself to bless the lives of others. Forgive me for the times I have failed to live
peaceably with those who touch my life. Create in me a clean heart and renew
the right spirit in me. Holy Spirit, help me to be diligent with my assignment
and to mind my own business. In Jesus' Mighty Name, Amen.

Reflections:

Based on this devotional entry, what are you trusting God for today?

Memory Verse: 1 Thessalonians 4:16 – 18 For the Lord Himself will descend from heaven with a loud cry of summons, with the shout of an archangel, and with the blast of the trumpet of God. And those who have departed this life in Christ will rise first. Then we, the living ones who remain [on the earth], shall simultaneously be caught up along with [the resurrected dead] in the clouds to meet the Lord in the air; and so always (through the eternity of the eternities) we shall be with the Lord! Therefore comfort and encourage one another with these words.

Thought for The Day: These Words Bring Hope!

---

*B*eing a leader in the Body of Christ throws you into the midst of the trials of others. One of the major concerns that must be regularly dealt with is the transition from earth into the eternal realm. None of us are thrilled to experience the departure of a loved one. We get sad just hearing about someone we don't even know having to deal with this part of life. Yet, we know from the moment we are able to comprehend death that it is surely coming our way. Not just for those we love, but for us, too!

In this passage of scripture we are told that Jesus will come from heaven with a loud announcement from His archangel and a deafening blast from the trumpet of God. There will not be a mistake about the time of His arrival. Those of us who have already departed the earth and are part of His Kingdom will be summoned first. After they have risen, those Believers who are still living on the earth shall be caught up, as well. It will be so quick our human comprehension will not be able to tell the difference. We will all be present with the Lord in the clouds. This will not be a momentary occurrence. We will forever be present with the

Lord! Eternity is a never-ending time of rejoicing. So when I am presented with the assignment of consoling someone who has had their heart torn by the departure of a loved one, this is one of the scriptures I like to refer to. Because we believe that Jesus died and rose again, we are comforted in knowing that the same thing will happen to us. Because we believe that's what's going to happen to us, we can believe that our loved ones will experience the resurrection, too. I like to remind those who have been left behind that they will never have to say goodbye to their loved one again. If their loved one believed the way they believe, they will spend eternity together. When someone has lived 70 + years, we say they have lived a long time and are blessed to have done so. Even if they have lived to be 100 or more years old, eternity means forever. We simply cannot comprehend the word "eternity." We are locked in time here on the earth, so we don't have the proper understanding of time never ending. The grieving of a Believer in the death of another Believer should not be the same as those who don't believe. We will experience pain, sadness, and ongoing grief. But we have hope beyond the grave. We have peace, because we believe that being absent from our physical body means that our spirit and soul are with the Lord. However, when He comes in the cloud, we will all receive our resurrected bodies as well! Even while we experience the natural emotion that comes with the loss of a loved one, we can find comfort in the Word of God, knowing that by faith, there is life after our brief time on this earth as we know it. These are the words I give to bring hope to a sad situation.

Declaration and Confession:

I believe that Jesus died and rose again! He has already made a way of escape from death to life and now, I have hope that will carry me into eternity with peace. What He did for me in His resurrection will happen to me as I will rise to meet Him in eternity. This peace surpasses my understanding and brings hope to others.

Prayer:

Dear Lord Jesus,

Thank you for making a way of escape for me. I don't have to fear death or grieve as others do, because I know that you're coming back for me. Help me to represent you well while I'm on this earth. I want to bring hope to those who don't know you so they too can experience resurrected life. In Jesus' Mighty Name, Amen.

Reflections:

Have you suffered the loss of a loved one? It really hurts to say goodbye, but these words bring hope! Receive them and rejoice!

Memory Verse: Isaiah 43:18, 19, 25, 26 Do not [earnestly] remember the former things; neither consider the things of old. Behold, I am doing a new thing! Now it springs forth, do you not perceive and know it and will you not give heed to it? I will even make a way in the wilderness and rivers in the desert. I, even I, am He Who blots out and cancels your transgressions, for My own sake, and I will not remember your sins. Put Me in remembrance [remind Me of your merits], let us plead and argue together. Set forth your case, that you may be justified (proved right).

Thought For the Day: Wite Out!

O ver twenty years ago, I had an electric typewriter that I thought I would never stop using. It was top of the line and had some features that made it unique. You could type some lines or a whole page, push a button, and it would retype whatever you had just typed. It also had a delete button that would take out your mistakes by backspacing over them. During that same time period, there was a popular product on the market called, "Wite Out!" It's a correction fluid that takes out your mistakes when you are writing something. The fact that it's white causes it to disappear along with your mistake, when used on white paper. Because of the computer age, "Wite Out!" is not needed as it once was. We can easily delete our mistakes when we are composing. Every now and then, we have a hard copy that needs correction, so "Wite Out!" can be used. This passage of scripture reminded me of this product, because the red blood of Jesus blots out all of our sins and cleanses us white as snow.

Just as "Wite Out!" is an old product and has been replaced by the delete button on the keyboard of our computers, God wants us to move on to what's happening today in our lives. He is a progressive God and is interested in the events of the day we are currently in. Looking back at our past mistakes keeps us from moving forward in the things He has for us today. Once we have asked for forgiveness, He wants us to take Him at His Word that says; He is faithful and just to forgive us and to cleanse us of all unrighteousness. Not accepting His forgiveness causes us to stumble on a mistake that is no longer there. It tells God that we don't trust His Word to be true. Actually, we are calling Him a liar. God is not a man that He should lie. So, the sooner we accept His ability to blot out our transgressions, the sooner we can accept the new things He has for us to do and the new blessings He has for us to receive. If we would just move forward in our thinking, accept God's mercy and forgiveness and agree with Him, our words and our actions would match His desires for our life and we would receive His Grace to complete His assignment for our lives. Although I told a friend of mine I would never stop using my typewriter when she urged me to start using the computer, I am thankful that I finally gave in and did what she suggested. The advantages of the computer far outweigh what my old typewriter could do. Now, I am able to complete more writing than I would have on my old typewriter. Likewise, God simply deletes our mistakes from the pages of our life. Our hard copies have already been corrected. We can move forward with what God has for us today and there's no further need for 'Wite Out!"

Declaration and Confession:

I refuse to dwell on the things of my past. I want to be included in the things God is doing today. In order for that to happen, I must receive God's forgiveness for things I've done in the past. There's no need for "Wite Out!" He gives me a way of escape in my wilderness and brings water to my dry places. I agree with what God says about me!

Prayer:

Dear Father God,

Thank you for accepting the right in me and rejecting the wrong! I'm ready to move on to the new things you have for my life. The blood of Jesus cleanses me, so I am free. I receive what you've put in me. In Jesus' name, Amen.

Reflections:

What can wash away our sins? Nothing but the precious blood of our Savior, Jesus Christ!

Memory Verse: 2 Corinthians 3:15 – 17 Yes, down to this [very] day whenever Moses is read, a veil lies upon their minds and hearts. But whenever a person turns [in repentance] to the Lord, the veil is stripped off and taken away. Now the Lord is the Spirit, and where the Spirit of the Lord is, there is liberty (emancipation from bondage, freedom).

Thought for the Day: You May Now Kiss Your Bride!

Most women love a good wedding and I happen to be one of those women. Although I was not in a hurry to get married as a young adult, I still liked to go to weddings. We love everything about it! The dreaming or imagining that goes with it. All the planning that involves picking a beautiful dress, choosing the colors, making sure the venue has a romantic setting, the elegance of the invitations, and who will be invited. This 30-minute to an hour ceremony has to be perfect! However, it's the reception or after party that costs the most and lasts the longest. We get to congratulate the bride and groom while mingling with the invited guests. There is excitement in the air and everyone is ready to celebrate the new union!

This scripture reminded me of a wedding ceremony because before a couple gets married they often have a minimal knowledge of who the other person really is. Although they've made a relationship commitment, they really have no idea of what they are committing to. Because the veil is still in place, they are blinded to the true meaning of marriage. However, after the party is over they become intimate with their mate on every level and find out exactly what they have signed up for. While dating, they may not have revealed all there is to know about themselves, but marriage will reveal it all: the good, the bad, and the ugly. If it's a good marriage they find out that the good outweighs the bad and they are blessed beyond measure. Choosing not to make the commitment of marriage would have deprived them of a wonderfully beneficial relationship.

Just as the newlyweds are about to embark on a new way of life, so does a newborn Christian. As long as we are operating under the mandates of the law given by Moses, we are not truly free. Before we accept what Christ did on the cross, we are doomed to the penalties of the law. Our hearts and minds are closed off from the reality of who Jesus really is. Deciding to repent of our sins, turn our lives over to Jesus, and becoming His bride brings us into a new way of living life. When we make that commitment the veil between the bride and the groom are ripped off. We have free access to the King of Kings and Lord of Lords! Although we don't know what we have really committed to, we are about to learn what living is really about. The Word of God is our guide into this new way of life and the Holy Spirit empowers us to live it successfully. We are the bride of Jesus Christ! He is married to us and has destroyed the veil that was between us. We have free access to all of the promises that He made to His bride. We are no longer in bondage to the law because where the Spirit of the Lord is, there is liberty! So the next time you go to a wedding and the groom lifts the veil of his bride as the minister says "you may kiss your bride," remember this and get ready to celebrate. You are the bride of Jesus Christ!

Declaration and Confession:

I have decided to commit my life to Jesus Christ. I am no longer under the bondage of the law. The blood of Jesus has set me free from the law of sin and death. I am the bride of Christ!

Prayer:

Dear Lord Jesus,

Thank you for accepting me as your bride! You took away the veil that prevents me from knowing you intimately. Now, I am free to know you completely. I love You and adore You. In Jesus' Mighty Name, Amen.

Reflections:

We are the bride of Christ, as His body. Have you kissed Him today?

Memory Verse: Psalms 90:1, 4, 10, 16, 17 Lord, You have been our dwelling place and our refuge in all generations [says Moses]. For a thousand years in Your sight are but as yesterday when it is past, or as a watch in the night. The days of our years are three score years and ten (seventy years) — or even, if by reason of strength, fourscore years (eighty years); yet is their pride [in additional years] only labor and sorrow, for it is soon gone, and we fly away. Let Your work [the signs of Your power] be revealed to Your servants, and Your [glorious] majesty to their children. And let the beauty and delightfulness and favor of the Lord our God be upon us; confirm and establish the work of our hands — yes, the work of our hands, confirm and establish it.

Thought for the Day: Faith Dictates to Time!

It has been said: "Time flies, when you're having fun!" Actually, time flies, whether you're having fun or not! God dropped us into a world ruled by time. Yet, He operates in the realm of eternity, which means He is not ruled by time. One day to Him is as a thousand years and a thousand years as one day. So, it is important that I don't allow time to cancel the promises of God for me. As I get older, I feel the urgency to get things done before my time runs out. At the same time, I must trust God to accomplish what He has given me to do in the time that He has ordained it to happen.

Each of us is allotted time here on earth and our time varies according to what our assignment is and how we respond to it. Jesus was here for what we consider to be a short time, but He accomplished what God had sent Him here to do. He was born into the earth to redeem mankind from death, hell, and destruction! We are so thankful for what He did!

As followers of Christ, we are here to reinforce what He has already accomplished in the earth. We may be here 70, 80, or 120 years, but that's not what's important. We want to do the work that He has sent us here to do, before our night comes and we are unable to complete our assignment. Although God is a patient God and allows us to learn from our mistakes, we must learn those lessons well and move on to glorifying God with our lives. We really want the light of Christ to shine through us, causing our generations to recognize the power of God working in us. We want our faith in God to bring hope to those around us. We want to live the length of our days giving praise to the God who has allowed us to represent Him during the time that we are here. He does not move according to our time, but in the time that He has ordained for things to happen. So we may as well operate as if there is no given time, because with God there isn't. His time is always the right time! Our faith in Him dictates to time just what time it is!

Declaration and Confession:

I am thankful for the time God has given to me! I am determined to stay in line with His timing for things. I put my trust in the All Wise, All Knowing God I serve. He gives me the courage to face each day knowing that He has time under control. My faith in Him dictates to time what time it is!

Prayer:

Dear Lord Jesus,

Teach me to number my days in line with your perfect will for my life. Give me the wisdom I need to make right choices during my stay in the earth. Holy Spirit, help me to yield to the timing of the Lord and to be an example to the generations that follow me. Let your favor confirm and establish the works of my hands. In Jesus' Mighty Name, Amen.

Reflections:

Have you thought about the timeline God has for your life? Let your faith dictate to time.

Memory Verse: Proverbs 24:3 – 5 Through skillful and godly wisdom is a house (a life, a home, a family) built, and by understanding it is established [on a sound and good foundation]. And by knowledge shall its chambers [of every area] be filled with all precious and pleasant riches. A wise man is strong and is better than a strong man, and a man of knowledge increases and strengthens his power.

Thought for the Day: Godly Knowledge Increases Strength!

---

*H*ave you ever looked at the body of an individual who has muscles popping out all over the place and thought it would be nice to be built like that? Nowadays, our society is mesmerized by those who have bodies that are really built. If the person is a woman, we want to have hair, a bust line, waistline, hips, and legs that would be envied by every other woman and lusted after by every man. If the person's a man, we want to have muscles, a six pack, sexual prowess, position, power, and money to foster great respect from every man or woman in our sphere of influence. Initially, we are high on the outward appearances of others, but in the end how they think, what they say, and how they act replaces or verifies our initial thought. In other words, "you can't read a book by its cover!"

Scripture tells us that exercising our body profits a little, but spiritual training is useful and valuable in everything (1 Timothy 4:8). We need a solid foundation to build our life on so we can benefit now and in the future. No matter how much we exercise our physical body, gravity eventually pulls everything down. Placing our hopes and trust in the living God who preserves, maintains, and delivers us makes us rich - spirit, soul, and body! Sooner or later, a storm will hit our lives and we will have to stand on the promises of God to survive. If we have not established every area of our life in the things of God, we will sink in the midst of the storm. If we operate in the wisdom of God, we will escape the winds of adversity and the floods against our soul. God desires that we be knowledgeable, not ignorant. So His Word is here for us to read, deposit, and apply. He has placed men and women in the earth to proclaim His Word, so we can hear the Word. Hearing the Word physically and spiritually brings faith our way. With faith, we can please God and have great success. Ultimately, our knowledge of God and how He operates gives us wisdom. That wisdom overrides our natural knowledge. We can have all kinds of educational awards and still have a dysfunctional life. No matter how wonderful we look on the outside, it's what's on the inside controlling the outside that counts. Our physical appearance will eventually fade away, but the Word of God will stand forever. It is our Godly knowledge that increases our strength!

Declaration and Confession:

When I increase my knowledge of God and His goodness and grace, my strength increases! Although I need to exercise my physical body, I will spend the majority of my time in spiritual training. It is useful and valuable in having a successful life. The Word of God that I hear and apply increases my faith. With that faith, I will please God! I ask God for wisdom to trust, rely on, and obey Him. The power and strength of God resides in Me!

Prayer:

Dear Father God,

Thank you for the wisdom you give me through Your Word! The Greater One in me helps me to understand Your will and Your way. The more I know about

You, the better my life will be. I desire to be free in Jesus, my Savior, my Lord! My strength comes from knowing You! In Jesus' Mighty Name, Amen.

Reflections:

How often do you work out in the Word of God? Remember, the strength of your inner man is more important than your outward appearance.

Memory Verse: Acts 12:5, 13 – 16 So Peter was kept in prison, but fervent prayer for him was persistently made to God by the church (assembly). And when he knocked at the gate of the porch, a maid named Rhoda came to answer. And recognizing Peter's voice, in her joy she failed to open the gate, but ran in and told the people that Peter was standing before the porch gate. They said to her, You are crazy! But she persistently and strongly and confidently affirmed that it was the truth. They said, It is his angel! But meanwhile Peter continued knocking, and when they opened the gate and saw him, they were amazed.

Thought for the Day: Rhoda Dared to Believe!

If it wasn't so sad, this would be a comical story! It really reveals our human nature, even as Believers. King Herod was really doing his thing to subdue the first Christians and had just killed James. To further please the Jews, he arrested Peter and put him in prison surrounded by 16 soldiers. His plan was to bring him before the people after the Passover. However, the Church prayed fervently for him to be delivered from the hands of Herod. Their prayers were so powerful that an angel was sent to rescue him the night before he was to face Herod. Although he was sleeping between two soldiers, fastened with two chains, and guarded by all the soldiers in front of the door; the angel woke him and led him passed those guards and the two guards in front of the exit doors leading to the city. After they were a distance from the prison, the angel disappeared and Peter continued to the house of Mary, the mother of John Mark. This was where the praying Christians were assembled.

When the angel showed up to rescue him, Peter thought he was having a vision. He did not realize that what was actually happening to him until after the angel left. Once the reality of God's intervention set in, he proclaimed that the Lord had sent an angel to deliver him from the hand of Herod and the Jews. He proceeded to the house of the assembled Believers. Once he got there, he knocked at the gate of the porch. Rhoda recognized his voice and got so excited that she forgot to answer the door! Full of joy because their prayers had been answered, she ran to tell the others. Instead of rejoicing with her and running to the gate to greet Peter, they told her she was crazy. That's typically how it is, we pray for things to happen, but because we deem our request to be so BIG, our level of expectancy is very low. We need to be like Rhoda and remain persistent and strong in our confidence that God hears and answers our prayers - no matter how monumental our ask may be, we must know that nothing is too hard for God to answer! It does not matter how crazy people may think we are. Even though they half-heartedly pray with us for our miracle, we must believe we receive what we pray for! The answer to their prayers was standing at the door! After they opened it and saw him in the flesh, they were still amazed. A minister who visited our church a long time ago entitled his message on this scripture, "What's Wrong with Rhoda?" and I never forgot it. My answer to his question is: "Rhoda Dared to Believe!"

Declaration and Confession:

I believe the fervent prayers of the righteous avail much! So when I make my request known to God, I expect to see the manifestation of my request. God is not a man that He would lie, so I believe His word concerning my victorious success. Therefore, I will exercise my faith and add it to my hope. If needed, God will assign an angel to aid in my rescue.

I can't afford to lean to my understanding, so I will allow God to direct my path to Victory! I believe, I receive, when I pray!

Prayer:

Dear Lord,

You have come to my rescue many times in the past. Therefore, I trust you to deliver me from the hands of my enemies. You have given me the keys to the Kingdom to bind and loose what is proper and improper in the earth. So, I will touch and agree with those who believe and stand ready to receive the Victory. In Jesus' Mighty Name, Amen.

Reflections:

Have you ever been shocked, when God answered your prayer? Be like Rhoda, dare to believe!

Memory Verse: John 8:44, 47 You are of your father, the devil, and it is your will to practice the lusts and gratify the desires [which are characteristic] of your father. He was a murderer from the beginning and does not stand in the truth, because there is no truth in him. When he speaks a falsehood, he speaks what is natural to him, for he is a liar [himself] and the father of lies and of all that is false. Whoever is of God listens to God [Those who belong to God hear the words of God.] This is the reason that you do not listen [to those words, to Me], because you do not belong to God and are not of God or in harmony with Him.

Thought of the Day: Who Do You Belong To?

---

*H*ave you ever heard the saying, "The apple doesn't fall far away from the tree?" That's what this scripture reminds me of. As I get older, I'm often told I look just like my mother. Not only do I look like her, many of her attributes are apparent in my mannerisms and lifestyle. When you are raised in a household, whether there are good or bad examples for life, you tend to pattern your life after your parents or guardians. Sometimes you gain good qualities and sometimes you learn bad habits. Eventually, you have to determine for yourself which pathway is best for you. Ultimately, we have the right to choose and can change our destiny based on who we want to pattern our life after.

In this passage of scripture, the religious leaders of the day kept saying they belonged to Father Abraham. Yet, they did not believe the way Abraham believed. When Abraham lived on the earth, He believed and trusted in God. He was an obedient child of God. Therefore, true descendants of Abraham believed God, too. They were talking about their natural blood line of Jewish descent but Jesus was talking about their spiritual heritage. He told them that true children of Abraham would do the works of Abraham by following his example. Being a child of God would cause you to love the truth and believe the truth. The fact that they were ready to kill Him because He claimed to be the Son of God was proof that they were not of God. He told them they would love, respect, and welcome Him if they were really of God and Abraham. Jesus was so confident in who He was that He boldly identified them with their real father, the devil. The one who came to steal, kill, and destroy! The one who operates in deceit and falsehood, he is the father of lies. If we profess to be children of God, we will love, respect, and welcome His Son! Our works will match the works He did when He was on the earth. His attributes of loving and believing the truth will be evident in us. Whether our natural parents chose lifestyles patterned after God or not, we have the right to choose the spiritual seed of Abraham or the corruptive seed of the devil. I choose to live a life that is patterned after the things of my Father God! I want my spiritual ears tuned into what He has to say. I try daily to walk in harmony with Him. We must all ask ourselves the question: who do I belong to?

Declaration and Confession:

I choose to eat from the tree of life! I will not swallow the lies of the enemy. I love, respect and welcome God's words of truth. I am part of the household of faith. Jesus is my Savior and Lord! I do His great and mighty works in the earth.

Prayer:

Dear Lord God,

Thank you for accepting me into your family! You are Abba, daddy to me. I listen to Your Spirit. He lives on the inside of me! When the world tries to steal or change my identity, I remember who I belong to. I belong to you: God the Father, and I believe what You have to say about me. I am complete in my identity with Jesus Christ, my Lord! In Jesus' Mighty Name, Amen.

Reflections:

Who does your lifestyle resemble? You have heavenly heritage. Pattern your life after your Father.

Memory Verse: 1 Corinthians 10:13 For no temptation (no trial regarded as enticing to sin), [no matter how it comes or where it leads] has overtaken you and laid hold on you that is not common to man [that is, no temptation or trial has come to you that is beyond human resistance and that is not adjusted and adapted and belonging to human experience, and such as man can bear]. But God is faithful [to His Word and to His compassionate nature], and He [can be trusted] not to let you be tempted and tried and assayed beyond your ability and strength of resistance and power to endure, but with the temptation He will [always] also provide the way out (the means of escape to a landing place), that you may be capable and strong and powerful to bear up under it patiently.

Thought for the Day: A Way of Escape!

Although God can use any experience to better our condition and relationship with Him, He does not use them to tempt us. He already knows what we can bear and what we cannot bear. This is not a guessing game for Him! Sometimes, things are brought our way and our right to choose causes us to make the wrong decision. Even if we do make a mistake, God will not allow anything to come into our life that we, by His grace and strength, don't have the capacity to withstand. He knows what's in us and what we can endure. He made the necessary deposits in us for us to obtain victory.

How awesome is that? God is so compassionate toward us that He always has a way out of whatever comes to wreck our world. It would be unfair for Him to allow something to come our way that we could not resist. If it's coming our way, we have the ability to resist. At the same time, He loves us enough to release us to make our own choices. He loves us enough to give us the power needed to endure. He has the answer key for every test we take during our life. All we have to do is request access to the key. Right now, I encourage you to begin to thank God for access to the answer key! When we're in the middle of a trial, it can feel like we're the only one who has to put up with what we are faced with. However, the truth is others have or are facing the same kind of problem. As human beings, there is nothing that has come our way that hasn't come someone else's way. There is nothing new under the sun. Yet, the pattern for each of our lives is different and unique and God has a particular plan for each one of our lives. We choose the way we want to handle His plan for us. In the end, it's always easier if we get in tune with Him and follow His directions. He wants us to submit to Him willingly. He will not force anything on us. We are free will agents. He knows that He has placed everything in us that we need to succeed. It's up to us to choose who and what we will serve on a daily basis. Wouldn't it be wonderful if we would always choose His way of escape?

Declaration and Confession:

God has the answer to every one of my situations and circumstances. If I listen to Him, I can avoid calamity in my life. Even when I make a mistake and choose the wrong pathway, He will lead me to the escape route. I know that God does not tempt me because He has a perfect plan for my life. I will choose His way of escape!

Prayer:

Dear Father God,

Help me to submit to Your will and Your way. I know you have deposited in me all the things that are necessary for me to win. If I allow the Holy Spirit in me to lead the way, I will experience Your best in my life. Jesus shed His Blood to cover a multitude of my sins and I am grateful. Yet, I want to live each day in a way that pleases You. Even in the time of trouble, help me to seek the way of escape you have planned for me. In Jesus' Mighty Name, Amen.

Reflections:

Do you feel powerless and trapped? Jesus has provided You a way of escape. Seek His way out!

Memory Verse: Philippians 3:9 – 11 And that I may [actually] be found and known as in Him, not having any [self-achieved] righteousness that can be called my own, based on my obedience to the Law's demands (ritualistic uprightness and supposed right standing with God thus acquired), but possessing that [genuine righteousness] which comes through faith in Christ (the Anointed One), the [truly] right standing with God, which comes from God by [saving] faith. [For my determined purpose is] that I may know Him [that I may progressively become more deeply and intimately acquainted with Him, perceiving and recognizing and understanding the wonders of His Person more strongly and more clearly], and that I may in that same way come to know the power outflowing from His resurrection [which it exerts over believers], and that I may so share His sufferings as to be continually transformed [in spirit into His likeness even] to His death, [in the hope] That if possible I may attain to the [spiritual and moral] resurrection [that lifts me] out from among the dead [even while in the body].

Thought for the Day: Dead Man Walking!

When I think about all the times I have failed to carry out to perfection the Laws presented by God in the Ten Commandments, I am so thankful for what Jesus did for me! I know He did it for you as well, but I know my own shortcomings and the times I have disappointed myself, not to mention the expectations of others. It is apparent that none of us are perfect, so it was expedient to our well-being that God sent Jesus to take our place. Without Him comings our earth to redeem us, we were doomed to eternal damnation. So I am grateful for the penalty of death being swallowed up by the Victory of Calvary's cross!

Because I don't have to depend on my ability to obey the Law, I can use my faith in Jesus Christ to obtain access to Almighty God and find grace to help me in every time of need. The penalty of death has been paid by the Blood of the Lamb. Jesus, the perfect sacrifice, has redeemed me from the curse of the law. The voice of the enemy or accuser of the brethren is silenced, because of the Blood that was shed for Me! Although he tries to keep my transgressions before me, I am innocent and have right-standing with God. That means I can cultivate a standing relationship with God and get to know Him intimately. I want to know everything there is to know about Him. He already knows everything about me. He knows the things I need to know about myself that will give me victory over the attacks of the enemy. The confidence and assurance I gain from knowing Him personally causes me to triumph over the deceptions of the enemy. The inside scoop about myself will keep me from falling into the traps set for me. The more I understand who I am in Christ Jesus, the more I'll be transformed into His image. To do that, I must die to self and the things of this world. I must lay down my life, resurrect, and become the person God wants me to be, the one that He has designed me to be. The same power that raised Jesus from the grave lives in me! So, as I surrender to the Father and resist the enemy and what he has to say about me, he will have to go in Jesus' name! Although my natural existence will have to die, the resurrection of my spiritual self will cause me to live in Victory! Then I can say I'm the Dead Man Walking!

Declaration and Confession:

I have inherited God's righteousness through Jesus Christ! As a result I have what it takes to obtain peace, security, and victory over all opposition of the enemy. My faith in what Jesus did on the cross gives me right-standing with Almighty God! I want to know Him intimately like He knows me. I choose to lay down my natural life to obtain supernatural living. Actually, you can say I am the Dead Man Walking!

Prayer:

Dear Lord Jesus,

Thank You for the Blood you shed on Calvary for me! It cleanses me from all unrighteousness and protects me from the attacks of the enemy. His accusations are null and void, because of what you did for me! As I seek to be more like you, I'll receive the victory! Thank You for redeeming me! In Jesus' Mighty name, Amen.

Reflections:

Have you been resurrected from the dead, even while you live?

Memory Verse: Mark 9:21 – 24 And [Jesus] asked his father, How long has he had this? And he answered, From the time he was a little boy. And it has often thrown him both into fire and into water, intending to kill him. But if You can do anything, do have pity on us and help us. And Jesus said, [You say to Me], If You can do anything? [Why,] all things can be (are possible) to him who believes! At once the father of the boy gave [an eager, piercing, inarticulate] cry with tears, and he said, Lord, I believe! [Constantly] help my weakness of faith!

Thought for the Day: Lord, Help My Unbelief!

How many times have you prayed for something miraculous to happen and failed to see it come to pass? I have prayed many times and have experienced both disappointment and what I deemed to be supernatural success. It's really hard to say what caused defeat and what caused victory. Each event had its own set of situations and circumstances. There are many factors involved in why things that we've prayed for have or have not manifested. The faith of the one being prayed for and the one doing the praying are major factors in the outcome of each situation. The key element in these situations is: "We walk by faith and not by sight!"

God's love for us is the one constant factor! He has our best interest at heart every time. So when we pray, we must believe that we receive what we pray for. The father in this story was desperate to have his son delivered from the torture he was experiencing on a daily basis. He knew that if this activity continued, his son would not survive. His son was being destroyed and it was breaking his heart to witness such torment.

He felt helpless and was fearful of the eventual outcome. Being a parent myself, I feel the pain that he was feeling concerning his son. His hope was that Jesus would be able to do something about his son's situation. All he really needed was faith to hook up with his hope, so their miracle could manifest. Jesus challenges him to change his expectation: "All things are possible!" He can, but do you believe he can? The father realized that the ball was in his court and he did not want to fail his son. So he said, "I believe, but if there is any doubt in me, please replace it with the faith I need to obtain victory." He wanted every trace of fear and doubt to leave. His son's life depended on it! So when we're facing an impossible situation, the only way we can expect the impossible to become possible is to have complete faith that ALL things are possible! God's love for us surpasses our human level of love. If this man found it hard to watch his son be destroyed and had the desire to see him set free, we know that the God who created him and loved him way beyond human love wanted him set free even more. Our complete faith and trust in a God who will not fail us is necessary. Lord, continually help our unbelief!

Declaration and Confession:

No matter how impossible things may look, I believe that ALL things are possible if I believe. I believe that God has my back! He knows what's best for me and if I can trust Him, He will provide everyone of my needs. I trust Him to do the impossible for me!

Prayer:

Father God,

You know what's best for me. I bring my needs and desires to you. I trust you to do what needs to be done on my behalf. Please replace all my doubts and fears with your supernatural faith to believe beyond what I can see. Thank you for giving me the Spirit of Power, Love, and a Sound Mind! In Jesus' Mighty Name, Amen.

Reflections:

Unbelief is a spirit. Send it away as far as the east is from the west!

Memory Verse: James 1:26, 27 If anyone thinks himself to be religious (piously observant of the external duties of his faith) and does not bridle his tongue but deludes his own heart, this person's religious service is worthless (futile, barren). External religious worship [religion as it is expressed in outward acts] that is pure and unblemished in the sight of God the Father is this: to visit and help and care for the orphans and widows in their affliction and need, and to keep oneself unspotted and uncontaminated from the world.

Thought of the Day: Soul Expressions!

When we accept Jesus as our Savior, a miracle in our spirit takes place. We become born again! Our spirit is recreated into the image of God. The DNA of the world is replaced with God's supernatural DNA. However, our soul (the place where our intellect, emotions, and will reside) is still programmed by the world. The only way we can erase all the things we have learned from living in this corrupt world is to study the Word of God. The Word of God has to replace the words of this world that are still stored in our soul.

It would be nice to have our souls instantaneously changed, but then there would be no voluntary submission on our part. In other words, we have an important part to play in our spiritual maturation. God wants us to line up our will with His perfect will for us. When He created mankind in the Garden of Eden, He placed us there with complete alignment. Our spirit, soul, and body were in total harmony with Him. Submitting to the serpent caused mankind to die and the soul became the boss of each of us. We were sold out to the kingdom of darkness. We gave Satan our position in ruling or having dominion in this world. Now, our acceptance of Jesus gives the Spirit of God access to our spirits. We allow Him to come into our being. Yet, our soul's salvation still has to be worked out. We have to allow the Spirit of God now in us to throw out all the unclean, wicked things that have been living in us. We have to submit our intellect, emotions, and will to God. We have to humbly replace our desires with God's desires. We must welcome the Word of God into our hearts to obtain the power it takes to override our soul. Once we do that, our actions will line up with the Word of God that is in our hearts. Then, we won't just proclaim God with religious rules and regulations. We will have the freedom to submit to the Word of God that is in our hearts. We won't be going through worthless motions of religious worship. We will allow the Spirit of God to control us on a daily basis. The words that come out of our mouths will line up with what's in our hearts. The love of God that's in our heart will come out through our mouths. We will redeem our God-given dominion. We will have God's desires in us to visit, help, and care for those who are in need of our assistance. The things the world has to offer will not be appealing to us. Our thoughts and emotions will be cleansed. Our bodies will submit to the part of us that dominates. We will truly be saved and restored with purified soul expressions!

Declaration and Confession:

I am determined to redeem my soul! Accepting Jesus into my life was just the beginning of my salvation experience. I want my thoughts, emotions, and will to line up with my born again spirit. I submit to the will and Word of God! My words are verbal expressions of God's love in me!

Prayer:

Dear Father God,

Thank you for saving me! Now, I must submit to Your will for my life. So I vow to study Your Word, so I won't sin against You. I choose to allow Your Spirit to align my spirit, soul, and body. Let the words of my mouth and the meditations of my heart be acceptable in Your sight. In Jesus' Mighty Name, Amen.

Reflections:

Examine your verbal expressions and make sure they line up with your Love for God.

Memory Verse: Psalm 95:6 – 8 O come, let us worship and bow down, let us kneel before the Lord our Maker [in reverent praise and supplication]. For He is our God and we are the people of His pasture and the sheep of His hand. Today, if you will hear His voice. Harden not your hearts as at Meribah and as at Massah in the day of temptation in the wilderness,

---

Thought for the Day: Why Wander?

It amazes me to think about all the times we argue with God! Instead of worshipping Him for all of the things He has done for us and thanking Him for being Our Creator, we spend an awful amount of time telling Him what we want Him to do. He is the Good Shepherd who knows all about His sheep. So it really isn't too smart of us to try to tell Him what to do. He already knows what we need to do in His pasture. We really act like silly sheep!

So today, I just want to take the time to bow down to a God who is lovingly patient with us. We say He is Our Shepherd and we shall not want, but we are constantly whining. Many times we find ourselves asking for the opposite of what He's given us. We find it hard to be satisfied with His provisions. Just like the children of Israel who complained instead of being grateful, we forget who God is! He proved over and over during their stay in the wilderness that He was there to take care of them. He provided for every one of their needs for 40 years. Yet, shortly after He would provide for them, they would accuse Him of neglect. They made Moses' job a miserable task for him! The sad thing is, we haven't learned from their mistakes. We grieve the hearts of our leaders and tempt them to sin against God out of frustration in trying to serve us. We really need to consider softening our hearts with the love of God and appreciate His provision. Even if it doesn't come in the way we want or through the person we desire. We need to open up our ears and listen to the voice of God through whatever instrument He sends it! We need to stop testing the patience of everyone around us! We make an easy journey hard. We break the heart of God with our disobedience and cause punishment to come our way. I believe I'll rest in the things God has for me and take the path of least resistance. It doesn't make sense to be lost, because I have the number one navigation system in me. So, why wander?

Declaration and Confession:

I have respect for God! He is the Good Shepherd! He cares for His sheep and provides for us in every way. I can rest in His ability to take care of me. So I will allow Him to reside on the throne of my heart and submit myself to Him. I want the promises He has made to me. I hear His voice and will follow Him! I refuse to wander!

Prayer:

Dear Lord,

Forgive me for every time I have complained, when you love me and want what's best for me. I worship and adore you, because you are my Creator. I open up my heart and listen to your voice. I praise you for who you are in my life. I will no longer have a quarrelsome attitude. You have already proven to me that you have the perfect plan for my life. So it would be to my advantage to seek you for direction. I want to enter into the Promised Land. Why should I wander, when you have the unique plan for my victory? Help me to be content in whatever state I'm in. I bow before you and give you all praise. In Jesus' Mighty Name, Amen.

Reflections:

Let's stay on course and follow the path God has set for us each day.

Memory Verse: Matthew 5:16 Let your light so shine before men that they may see your moral excellence and your praiseworthy, noble, and good deeds and recognize and honor and praise and glorify your Father Who is in heaven.

Thought for the Day: I Bring Light to the Subject

We all know about the purpose of a lighthouse. It is a tower with a bright light on top to guide ships at night or in a fog. This keeps the ships from getting lost at sea. When they see the lighthouse, they know that they are getting close to the safety of the shore. If the light in the lighthouse were out for some reason, the ships would be subject to calamity. The light at the top of the tower does not make a sound. It just shines and is a dependable beacon of hope.

As children of God, we are supposed to be the light of the world. We should be a light on a hill that is not hidden, or a lamp that is not under a basket. The light is there for all to see. It's one thing to talk the talk, but a completely different matter to walk the walk. People, saved and unsaved, should be able to see the light of Jesus Christ in our lives. If the Greater One really lives in us, then His presence should be visible in our daily walk here on earth. Our good character and high moral standards should be something people brag on us for. They should say we are people of excellence in all we say and do. We're on a journey and they should see a smile on our face and feel the joy in our hearts, letting them know we're enjoying the trip. We shouldn't be about doom and gloom. It may be the middle of the night in their life's situation or circumstance and they may not be able to see their way, because of the fog in their mind causing them to be confused and bewildered. People should be inspired to come to us, because they know we can bring light to the subject of life they are presently dealing with. How do they know that? Because they have seen us stand still and see the salvation of the Lord in the storms of life we have faced. They have witnessed the confidence we have in God to speak to the mountains and see them move in our life. The word of our testimony has proven that we are a dependable light, shining in the darkness for all to see. Believing the lies of the enemy could cause me to think that my light isn't important and I could be the cause of calamity in someone's life who was depending on me to be a strong tower. God has brought us out of darkness into His marvelous light. So allow your light to shine so men may see your good works and honor and glorify your Father in heaven. Let's put some light on the subject!

Declaration and Confession:

I decree and declare, right now, that the light of Jesus that is in me will shine brightly, as I allow the power of the Holy Spirit to regenerate it daily. I am a strong tower, a beacon of hope to those who are lost or in a storm that life has brought their way. I know how to speak "peace be still" to the winds and waves in my own life. I am steadfast, unmovable, always abounding in the work of the Lord! I will not allow satan to put out my light with his lies and deception. I vow to bring light to the subject of life!

Prayer:

Dear Lord Jesus,

You showed us how to handle the storms of life, as you traveled here on earth. Your compassion and love for others was evident and you were a strong tower for them. Please help me to be the light, shining in the darkness for all to see, as I journey through this life. I want to be a beacon of hope to others and victorious in the midnight hour of my own situations and circumstances. Thank you for using me to be a light that brings honor, glory, and praise to my heavenly Father. In Jesus' name, Amen.

Reflections:

Is your light shining for Jesus? What happens when you enter into a situation or circumstance of darkness?

Memory Verse: Proverbs 18:20, 21 A man's [moral] self shall be filled with the fruit of his mouth; and with the consequence of his words he must be satisfied [whether good or evil]. Death and life are in the power of the tongue, and they who indulge in it shall eat the fruit of it [for death or life]. (Matthew 12:34-37)

Thought for the Day: It's Your Mouth!

One of the hardest things for us to do is to shut our mouth! There have been times that I could hear the Holy Spirit say to me, "don't say it," but out of my mouth it would come. What exactly was coming out of my mouth? If the Holy Spirit said not to say it, then it was something I had no business saying. Many of us don't like to be around people who say curse words. It just sends chills up our back to hear others swearing. We think to ourselves, "I wish these swearing people would watch what comes out of their mouth." It just isn't necessary to be cursing like that. We're quick to judge people who do that. Certain words just don't sit right with us. When someone says those words, our face gets a look of disgust on it and the people say, "What's wrong?" We're quick to say, "It's that mouth of yours!"

Well, what does God think about the words that come out of our mouth? They may not be those words that we dislike, but they may be words God dislikes. When we have a bad attitude and complain about everyone and everything around us, curse words will follow our attitude. If we are ungrateful and self-centered, our mouth will bring forth words of selfishness and discontentment. If we fail to forgive others, our words will be words of bitterness and resentment. If we think we know everything and no one can tell us anything, our words will be full of arrogance and self-righteousness. It we think thoughts that are based on the law, rather than grace; our words will be full of condemnation and legalism. In other words, if our hearts are full of evil thoughts, that's what's going to come out of our mouths. There are some people who are just mean and no one wants to be around them. They may not say one curse word, but talk about people and things in a hateful manner. Then, there are those that always find something good to say about people and find the good in every situation. They may be criticized because people think they're too good to be true. Nevertheless, it's more important for God to be satisfied than to satisfy other people.

We need to realize that we are going to be held accountable for the words that come out of our mouth. Our words have power and will bring forth life or death when they are spoken into the atmosphere. We are made in God's image and He spoke forth words that brought the things in this world to life. We have that same creative ability. So, we have to be careful about what we allow to be planted in our heart. Whatever is in our heart will bring forth the fruit that will come out of our mouth. A sweet kind person does not have mean, vindictive thoughts and a truly evil person does not have good, loving thoughts. So, good thoughts bring forth good fruit! Whatever is hidden in our hearts will sooner or later be expressed openly through our mouths. If there is unbelief in our hearts, that same unbelief will come out of our mouth in words of doubt and fear. These kinds of words are curse words to God. They produce negative results. They demonstrate doubt in His promises and power. If the Holy Spirit tells us not to say something, we had better listen and receive acquittal, so we won't be subject to sentencing by God and hear Him say, "It's your mouth!"

Declaration and Confession:

Holy Spirit, please put a bridle on my tongue. I want the words that come out of my mouth to be those that bless and not curse. My heart is filled with good, loving thoughts, so good things come out of my mouth. Wrong thoughts are not allowed to dwell in my heart. I eat the fruit of life and not death!

Prayer:

Dear Lord Jesus,

Please forgive me for every evil or idle thought that has been in my heart. Cleanse my heart and mind of those thoughts that are not pleasing to You. I pull down every strong hold in my mind. Help me to say words of faith, love, and peace that honor You. I cancel all negative thoughts and desires, by Your Spirit. Thank you Lord for a clean heart and a right spirit! In Jesus' Mighty Name, Amen.

Reflections:

What do you allow to come out of your mouth? Make a conscious effort to submit to the Holy Spirit, when it comes to your mouth.

Memory Verse: Acts 2:1 – 4 And when the day of Pentecost had fully come, they were all assembled together in one place. When Suddenly there came a sound from heaven like the rushing of a violent tempest blast, and it filled the whole house in which they were sitting. And there appeared to them tongues resembling fire, which were separated and distributed and which settled on each one of them. And they were all filled (diffused throughout their souls) with the Holy Spirit and began to speak in other (different, foreign) languages (tongues), as the Spirit kept giving them clear and loud expression [in each tongue in appropriate words].

Thought for the Day: Suddenly!

I really want to share with you about what was the greatest key to my personal walk with God. It was something that happened to me suddenly! Many years ago, I was trying to figure out why I felt I had hit a glass ceiling spiritually? I was very active in my local church and had various responsibilities of leadership that I was involved in. Yet, singing in the choir, working with the women's group, and assisting with the youth department didn't seem to be quenching my thirst for more. I really didn't have any more hours to give in service to my church, so I was puzzled about how I was feeling. In my search for the solution to my problem, I landed right in the middle of one of the major controversies of the Body of Christ. It all began with my discovery concerning the Holy Spirit.

Suddenly, I found myself thrust in the middle of a wilderness experience. Just as Jesus was after He was baptized by John the Baptist in water and the Spirit of God descended on Him like a dove. When God declared that, "This is My beloved Son, in whom I am well pleased," The Spirit of God led Him into the wilderness to be tempted by the devil. I can't even begin to tell you all of the things the devil brought my way after I received the baptism of the Holy Spirit. Now, that I can look back on what I went through with the help of the Holy Spirit, I know God was pleased with my decision to follow in the footsteps of Jesus. Had I known what I was about to go through, I may not have had the courage to choose that day. However, the statement "ignorance is bliss" may apply to this particular situation. I didn't know what I was doing. I was just blindly following the leading of the Holy Spirit. Now, I am so glad I did! The void I had felt in my heart was now filled. I no longer felt that I was going nowhere fast. I was on a lifelong adventure that I wouldn't trade for anything. Did it cost me? Yes, it did! Jesus gave His whole life so that I could experience an intimate relationship with His Father. If He was willing to give His life, so I could have a life, I need to be willing to give mine, as well. Being filled to the brim with the Holy Spirit keeps me in the presence of God, helps me overcome life's challenges with peace and wisdom, and makes it difficult for the enemy and the mentality of the world to influence me.

Suddenly, my hunger and thirst for the Word increased. I began to saturate my soul with biblical information by reading the Word, which I already did, but now I was getting revelation knowledge of what I was reading by the Holy Spirit. Suddenly, my prayer life completely changed! Because I could use my prayer language or speak in tongues, I had immediate access to the throne room of God. The devil could not interrupt my communication with God. He didn't know what I was saying and neither did I, but the Spirit of God did. The Spirit of God knows exactly how to pray and what to pray for. The more I put this spiritual tool to work the more I was able to pray in English with the same fervor I did in tongues. Eventually, my spirit was given interpretation from the Holy Spirit and that increased my understanding even more. Suddenly, I was able to pour into the lives of other people and give them sound biblical information. Suddenly, I had confidence in my personal relationship with God. Jesus became Lord of my life! The Holy Spirit empowered me to do spiritual exploits! Suddenly, I was on a spiritual adventure that has not stopped yet and I don't want it to! So, come on and join me in experiencing, suddenly!

Declaration and Confession:

I am a Spirit-filled Believer! My soul is energized and disciplined by the Holy Spirit within me! He subdues by tongue, so I speak out the right words. He causes me to speak life rather than death filled words. The Word of God is made clear to me. The gifts of the Spirit flow freely through me! I love my Pentecostal experience!

Prayer:

Dear Lord,

You are an Awesome God! Thank you for allowing me to experience YOU, Suddenly! In Jesus' Mighty Name, Amen.

Reflections:

Have you had your "Suddenly" experience? If not, seek the Holy Spirit, ask for your "suddenly", and you shall receive.

Memory Verse: Joshua 1:8, 9 This Book of the Law shall not depart out of your mouth, but you shall meditate on it day and night that you may observe and do according to all that is written in it. For then you shall make your way prosperous, and then you shall deal wisely and have good success. Have not I commanded you? Be strong, vigorous, and very courageous. Be not afraid, neither be dismayed, for the Lord your God is with you wherever you go.

Thought for the Day: Be Bold, Be Strong!

Years ago there was a song with these words:
Be Bold, Be Strong, for the Lord thy God is with you! I am not afraid, I am not dismayed, because I'm walking in Faith and Victory, come on and walk in Faith and Victory; for the Lord thy God is with you!

I use to love that song, because it encouraged me to believe the Word of God that we're focusing on today. Joshua and Caleb were the only two spies out of 10 who were bold enough to come back with a good report. They believed that with God on their side, they were able to possess the land God had promised to them. The other spies compared themselves to grasshoppers that would be squashed by the giants of the land.

Now that Moses had died, the baton was being passed to Joshua to lead the Israelites into the Promise Land. God promised him that He would be with him, just like He was with Moses. He told Joshua He would not fail or forsake him. He told him to be Strong and Very Courageous. He told him not to turn to the left or right, but to stay on the path already set my Moses. Just as God told Joshua not to deviate from the Book of the Law, we need to stay on course with the Word of God. We need to hide it in our heart and meditate on it day and night. If we do, God will make our way prosperous, we will deal wisely, and have great success! It sounds simple and it is. All we have to do is study the Word of God and allow it to marinate in our heart or spirit. Then, we will be able to deal wisely with the things that occur in our lives and the lives we touch. Because we have the wisdom of God in us, we will make the right decisions. We will have godly thoughts that will bring godly results. We will bear much fruit. Our faith will increase and we will be able to do great exploits for God. Our life will be a life of Victory and Success! The only problem we have is to defeat the lies and thoughts of the enemy that will try to invade our mind and distract our focus. Instead of thinking of ourselves as grasshoppers, we have to think of ourselves as giant killers. We have to Be Bold, Be Strong, for the Lord Our God is with Us!

Declaration and Confession:

Because I have the Word of God in my heart, I have the power to Be Bold! Because God will never leave me or forsake me, I am Strong and Confident in pursuit of the things God has promised me! I am courageous, because I'm walking in Faith and Victory! I will not turn to the left or right, but I will keep my feet in the narrow path of righteousness! I am Bold as a lion and harmless as a dove. I am not afraid or dismayed. I know the Lord My God is with me wherever I go!

Prayer:

Dear Lord God,

I come to you with a humble heart. It's my desire to take Your Word seriously and hide it in my heart. Your Word gives me the strength I need to endure and defeat the giants in my life. The Greater One in me helps me to Believe Your Word and accept Your promises as mine. You have not given me a spirit of fear, but one of power, love, and a sound mine. I am bold and strong, because I put my trust in You. In Jesus' Mighty Name, Amen.

Reflections:

Do you believe that the Lord your God is with you? Be bold, be strong, because He is with you and that's the truth!

Memory Verse: 2 Kings 20:1-3, 5,6,11 In those days Hezekiah became deadly ill. The prophet Isaiah son of Amoz came and said to him, Thus says the Lord. Set your house in order, for you shall die, you shall not recover. Then Hezekiah turned his face to the wall and prayed to the Lord, saying. I beseech You, O Lord, [earnestly] remember now how I have walked before You in faithfulness and truth and with a whole heart [entirely devoted to You] and have done what is good in Your sight. And Hezekiah wept bitterly. Turn back and tell Hezekiah, the leader of My people. Thus says the Lord, the God of David your [forefather]: I have heard your prayer, I have seen your tears; behold, I will heal you. On the third day you shall go up to the house of the Lord. I will add to your life fifteen years and deliver you and this city [Jerusalem] out of the hand of the king of Assyria; and I will defend this city for My own sake and for My servant David's sake. So Isaiah the prophet cried to the Lord, and He brought the shadow the ten steps backward by which it had gone down on the sundial of Ahaz.

Thought for the Day: Turning Back the Hands of Time!

---

*T*his is a very powerful story! The New Testament tells us that the prayer of a righteous man avails much. So, we see in this account, the same principle being applied. Although it comes from the Old Testament, Hezekiah is a righteous man in the sight of God. He's given a bad report and told to get his house in order. Rather than accept that report, he prays, and God grants him his request. So, he gets a 15 year extension on his life.

Even though God had given him this promise; Hezekiah wants confirmation or a guarantee that the promise will be kept. The prophet Isaiah gives him a choice of having the shadow of the sundial move 10 steps forward or backward. Since Hezekiah thinks it is no big feat to have the shadow move forward, he makes the request to have it move backward. The prophet makes the request of God and the shadow moves 10 steps backward. In this dispensation, we have the inner witness of the Spirit of God, who is deposited in us to confirm things. At the time of this story, there was no inner witness, so God used an outer witness to confirm His promise to Hezekiah. Just as the prophet was used to assist in this confirmation in the story, sometimes the words from the prophet today are used to confirm the promises God has made to us. God goes to great lengths to assure us that He is ever present to hear our prayers. Because Hezekiah had been a faithful servant of God, he was able to make his request known to God. Jesus came so we can have direct access to God's ear. We don't have to have a prophet or a priest to do our bidding. If we receive a bad report, we can approach the throne of God boldly and expect to receive an answer. Whatever we have the faith to believe we can receive. There's nothing too hard for God, if we need Him to, He can turn back the hands of time on our behalf!

Declaration and Confession:

I believe in the power of God! If there is a situation that seems impossible in my life, I can go to God in prayer and expect an answer. My God hears and answers my prayers. I am the Righteousness of God in Christ Jesus! So, my prayers avail much. The Spirit of God in me gives me an inner witness to the promises of God!

Prayer:

Dear Father God,

Thank you for hearing and answering my prayers! I trust You with my life! Even with a bad report, I choose to live and not die. Yet, you know what's best for me. So, I will yield my will to your perfect will. I can lean and depend on You for the length of my days here on earth. Just let me run with endurance until I cross the finish line and hear You say, "Well done! My good and faithful servant." In Jesus' Mighty Name, Amen.

Reflections:

We serve an approachable God. You have access to boldly ask Him for whatever you need. Do it today!

Memory Verse: Isaiah 61:6-8 But you shall be called the priests of the Lord; people will speak of you as the ministers of our God. You shall eat the wealth of the nations, and the glory [once that of your captors] shall be yours. Instead of your [former] shame you shall have a two-fold recompense instead of dishonor and reproach [your people] shall rejoice in their portion. Therefore in their land they shall possess double [what they had forfeited]; everlasting joy shall be theirs. For I the Lord love justice; I hate robbery and wrong with violence or a burnt offering. And I will faithfully give them their recompense in truth and I will make an everlasting covenant or league with them.

Thought for the Day: "I Want Double!"

As a woman, I just love a good sale! And it's really not a sale to me unless the store is giving 50% or more off of its merchandise. Of course 50% means half, so I use to tell my 4th grade students to divide by 2 to find out what half of something is. Along the same lines of that thinking, multiplying by 2 gives you double. I believe that the wealth of the wicked has been laid up for the righteous. Those of us who proclaim to be Believers of Jesus Christ, even though we don't do everything right, have right-standing with God. What Jesus did for us is enough to put us in the right relationship with God! It's not based on us any longer. We belong to the Kingdom of God and Jesus is Lord of His Kingdom! So, everything the enemy has tried to steal from us over the years has been ransomed by what Jesus did on the cross. I am no longer in shame for the wrong I've done - and neither should you be. Jesus gave His life so we could receive eternal life. We get the reward of double for everything that was stolen from us. The enemy is accusing or blaming us for the wrong we've done, but Jesus has already purchased our reward for believing in Him! This is better than any sale I've been to, because no matter what percent they give off of the merchandise I want to buy, I'm still the one paying for it. The blood of Jesus covers my sins, so it's just as if I hadn't and He paid for it. To top that off, I get DOUBLE for my trouble! I think that's something to shout about! There's no way I could have done this for myself, because I was doomed from the start. So why don't you join me in enjoying the benefits of what Jesus has done for us! Although we had forfeited what God had originally given us in the Garden of Eden, Jesus has redeemed us from the curse and has made it possible for us to possess double! We can have double everlasting joy and peace! We have access to the truth and the truth we know will set us free. Satan is the thief who came to steal, kill, and destroy, but Jesus came that we would have abundant life. That means I have a covenant or blood earned agreement with God that gives me Double for my Trouble and so can you!

Declaration and Confession:

God, I have been chosen by You to be a priest because you have given me the ability to minister to others by Your Holy Spirit in me. I will eat the wealth of the nations and the glory that belonged to my captors shall be mine. I am no longer ashamed of my past, because Jesus has redeemed me from it. Instead, I will receive double for all of the trouble I have encountered in my life. I rejoice over all that You have done for me! I can depend on You, because You are a God of justice. You have taken care of the thief who came to steal from me. I receive Your reward of Truth in my life. I am bound by the blood covenant You have made with me!

Prayer:

Dear Lord Jesus,

Thank you for all you have done for me! I know I don't deserve it, but You chose to give your life for me. I receive your forgiveness for the wrong I've done. I know you have already forgiven me because You came to rescue me from the thief who came to steal my very life from me. Thank you for the love, joy, and peace you give to me. I receive Double for My Trouble. In Jesus' Mighty Name, Amen.

Reflections:

Based on this devotional entry, what are you trusting God for today?

Memory Verse: John 7:37 – 39 Now on the final and most important day of the Feast. Jesus stood, and he cried in a loud voice. If any man is thirsty, let him come to Me and drink! He who believes in Me [who cleaves to and trusts in and relies on Me] as the Scripture has said, From his innermost being shall flow [continuously] springs and rivers of living water. But he was speaking here of the Spirit, Whom those who believed (trusted, had faith) in Him were afterward to receive. For the [Holy] Spirit had not yet been given, because Jesus was not yet glorified (raised to honor).

Thought of the Day: "I'm Flowing Like A River!"

O ne thing about living in the desert, you don't enjoy the benefits of a lot of water. Here in New Mexico, you don't see much water. In fact, when it rains or snows, it is only for a very brief time. Then, the arrival of the sun dries it up so quickly that someone who didn't witness the rain - and sometimes even the snow! - for themselves would think you were lying about its visit two hours ago. We have a river called the Rio Grande. It means the great, large, or huge river. Most of the time, it looks like the large mud hole because there is not enough water in it for it to be considered a river. A river is usually a large natural stream of free-flowing water. It can flow into an ocean, lake, or another river. In the course of its flowing, it waters the shrubbery, rocks, debris, and anything or anyone that enters its pathway.

This describes the life of a Christian who not only possesses the well of living water inside of them, but they are also overflowing with the river of living water. These are the Believers of Jesus Christ, who have accepted Him as Savior and Lord of their lives. Their well is flooded with the living water that Jesus gives! They have been baptized by Jesus in the Holy Spirit! Everywhere they go their moisture enhances the atmosphere and dry lives of others. The outpouring of the Holy Spirit in them changes the negative situations and circumstances that are present. They never enter in and leave things stale and dry. Their journey in life affects the things they touch along the way. I strive to be this kind of Christian because I really don't want to be a mud hole! I don't want to be bogged down in the circumstances and situations of life. I want to be free flowing! I want to benefit the lives of those I touch. I want to bring the power of Jesus Christ into the atmosphere when I arrive. I want the Word of God to be rich in me! So join me: allow the Spirit of God to fill you to overflowing! Being a well of living water is not enough for me. I want to be a river of living water that flows into the ocean of all God has to offer and flows out again to be God's river of living water!

Declaration and Confession:

I am a river of living water. God's Spirit flows through me. I study His Word to benefit my life and get the wisdom I need to overcome situations and circumstances I encounter along my journey. Because I am a river, it is my desire to contribute to the lives of others in a positive way. I flow in the power of Jesus Christ by the overflow of His Spirit in Me. I allow Him to use me in a way that brings Victory into the atmosphere!

Prayer:

Dear Lord Jesus,

It's my desire to be a river of living water. Please baptize me in Your Holy Spirit as often as is needed. I want Your Spirit to affect my life to the point of overflow so I can be a blessing to the lives of others. Use me Lord, as an instrument of your service. Thank you for filling me! In Jesus' Name, Amen.

Reflections:

Which would you like to be, a well or a river of living water? It's all up to you!

Memory Verse: Proverbs 16:18, 19 Pride goes before destruction, and a haughty spirit before a fall. Better it is to be of a humble spirit with the meek and poor than to divide the spoil with the proud.

Thought for the Day: It's No Fun to Fall!

I think one of the hardest things to do is to recognize pride when it's operating in us. Many families have suffered loss because the wife or the husband or both won't let go of their pride. The cost of being right can be pretty expensive. Sometimes the children involved are the ones who really pay the price. Wouldn't it be nice if we could stand on the outside of ourselves and see what happens when we allow our pride to destroy our family, our job, our friendships, and most importantly our standing with God? Whenever it's our way or the highway, we are headed for a fall. Rather than admit that we are wrong or listen to someone else's point of view, we dig our heels in and allow the things that really count to be destroyed.

Sometimes what others call giving in is really being humble or doing what's better for everyone involved. Many times, getting what we want isn't what's best for the situation or circumstance. If we could lay aside our own way long enough to hear the voice of the Holy Spirit when there's conflict, we would be able to see what the best way should be. It would be great if we would allow the Spirit of God to rule and reign in the way we think. What if we allowed Him to be the final voice in our decision making? I believe things would have a much better outcome! If we would just trust the Spirit of God above our own thinking or feelings, whether we agreed or not, we would come out on top in every situation and circumstance. We would never be out of step with God, because we would depend on Him and trust Him to direct our path. We would depend on Him to see what we cannot see from our viewpoint. Therefore, we would have a definite advantage over the happenings of our life. Being submissive to God is a very good thing. It's being meek. The world considers meekness to be a spineless position. God sees it as being strong to be humble rather than boastful and proud. Every time we think more of ourselves than we should, we are headed for a big fall. It keeps us from thinking the way we need to think. Since we can't see everything and don't know everything, it would be best to listen to the Spirit of God who does. When He tells us we're setting ourselves up for a fall, we need to learn to listen. Most of us have already proven that pride keeps us from handling things the best way. Let's learn to humble ourselves because it's no fun to fall!

Declaration and Confession:

I want the best outcome possible in my life. So I choose to humble myself and listen to the voice of God. I will listen when He tells me I am thinking to high of myself. I will not operate according to my feelings either. I will submit to God's way of doing things. He has a better viewpoint and will keep me from falling.

Prayer:

Dear Lord God,

You know the beginning, middle, and end of my life. So I will listen to what you say over what I think or feel. My thoughts are not higher than yours. In fact, You have placed the Greater One on the inside of me. Therefore, Your Spirit that is in me knows how to keep me humble. If I allow You to keep me humble, You will exalt me when the time is right. I don't need to promote my own agenda. Thank You for showing me when I am wrong, because it's no fun to fall. In Jesus' Mighty Name, Amen.

Reflections:

Try eating some humble pie. It will cancel out the calamity of a fall.

Memory Verse: Genesis 16:3 – 5 So Sarai, Abram's wife, took Hagar her Egyptian maid, after Abram had dwelt ten years in the land of Canaan, and gave her to her husband Abram to be his [secondary] wife. And he had intercourse with Hagar, and she became pregnant; and when saw that she was with child, she looked with contempt upon her mistress and despised her. Then Sarai said to Abram, May [the responsibility for] my wrong and deprivation of rights be upon you! I gave my maid into your bosom, and when she saw that she was with child, I was contemptible and despised in her eyes. May the Lord be the judge between you and me.

Thought of the Day: Plan B!

---

*H*as God ever made you a promise or given you directions that don't seem to be coming to pass? When God makes us a promise, He is not a man that He should lie. What we need to do is have faith in His ability to perform what He says He will perform. Our timing is not His timing and our ways are not His ways. The Creator of the Universe ought to know what to do, when to do it, and how to do it. As human beings, we are impatient and have a hard time waiting on the promises of God to manifest. There are certain things that must come into play before He can do what He wants to do. We don't have the whole picture, so we get impatient and decide that Plan A is not working, so we come up with our own Plan B.

In this passage of scripture, we have Sarai usurping God's plan for her own. God had informed Abram of his plan to give him and Sarai a child from his own body for an heir. However, seeing that she had not bore any children and was an old woman, Sarai thought she would help God out. She decided that what God had promised Abram was not going to come to pass the way

He said. So she interfered with God's Plan A and instituted a Plan B. Her Plan B involved bringing her Egyptian maid to her husband to complete God's Plan A. Unfortunately, Abram made the same mistake Adam made and listened to his wife instead of God. So, Plan B was consummated and Sarai did not like the results. Her maid started making fun of her by flaunting her pregnancy. When we usurp God's authority in our lives to implement our own plan, we have to suffer the consequences of our actions. Sarai turned around and placed the blame on Abram for sleeping with her maid, even though it was her idea. That's the way we are, if we come up with something that doesn't work, we want to place the blame on someone else. After all, Abram was the head of the household and should have put his foot down on Sarai's request. Be real, Abram was just like any other man that would be presented an opportunity to check out another lady with his wife's permission. So, we can learn from their mistakes. God is the All Wise God who knows what He is doing and why He's doing it the way He chose to do it. If God gives you A Plan, don't substitute with your B Plan!

Declaration and Confession:

I believe the promises God makes to me! Sometimes it's hard for me to understand and it may not come in the time that pleases me. Nevertheless, I will be still and wait on God. The pledges He makes to me are accurate and true. I will not listen to the enemy, when he gives me Plan B to cancel out God's Plan A!

Prayer:

Dear Father God,

You know more about my life than I do. I trust You to give me the plan that will work for my life. If I follow your directions, things will work out the way they are supposed to. Because Your Spirit dwells in me, I have the ability to wait with patience on You. Thank You for the wisdom You have given to me, so I will make the right choices in life. Jesus followed Your plan, so I can have eternal life. I want to follow His example. In Jesus' Mighty Name, Amen.

Reflections:

Are you guilty of coming up with a Plan B, when God gives you a directive? Let's stick to God's plan and eliminate Plan B!

Memory Verse: 2 Corinthians 4:8 – 10, 15 We are hedged in (pressed) on every side [troubled and oppressed in every way], but not cramped or crushed, we suffer embarrassments and are perplexed and unable to find a way out, but not driven to despair; We are pursued (persecuted and hard driven), but not deserted [to stand alone]; we are struck down to the ground, but never struck out and destroyed; Always carrying about in the body the liability and exposure to the same putting to death that the Lord Jesus suffered, so that the [resurrection] life of Jesus also may be shown forth by and in our bodies. For all [these] things are [taking place] for your sake, so that the more grace (divine favor and spiritual blessing) extends to more and more people and multiplies through the many the more thanksgiving may increase [and redound] to the glory of God.

Thought for the Day: To the Glory of God!

We sing a song entitled "My Tribute" by Andre Crouch that has become an anthem for the Body of Christ. The lyrics, "to God be the Glory," tell us that everything we do in our lives as Believers should be attributed to the glorious finished work of Jesus Christ. We want to please Him because He gave His life for us. You really can't give any more than that. Because God was willing to send Jesus and He was willing to come, we owe all that we are and all that we have to them. We want to live our life to please them.

Even though we are pressed on every side because life happens, we are able to bounce back. Sometimes, we endure ridicule that brings us great embarrassment or are confused about what to do in some situations and circumstances. Yet, we know that in the end God will work things out for us. So we don't give up our hope. Although it may feel like we are all alone, we have to make a stand for something. We know deep down inside, we are not alone. The velocity of the fiery dart that is sent our way may cause us to fall to the ground, but our shield of faith will quench it and give us victory. Just as Jesus was tempted and challenged concerning His loyalty to God His Father, so are we. We have to make the choice daily to put our natural desires to death and allow the Spirit of the Living God to rule supreme in our life. It's the divine favor and spiritual blessings of God that makes the difference in our lives. As others watch how we live and maintain victory in the challenges of life. The Word of God comes alive in our daily activities. They can see that there is a reality in serving the Living God. As we show the love of God to those around us, they want what we have. So when they ask us what causes us to live in victory, all we can say is, "To God Be the Glory!"

Declaration and Confession:

Although I face troubles and may be pressed on every side, I am not crushed! Some of the things I endure in life may bring embarrassment my way, but I know who I am in Jesus Christ! I may not know what to do in some situations and circumstances, but I know who to call for help. I am full of hope, because divine favor is coming my way. Even in the midst of opposition, I am not alone! The Greater One in me gives me the Victory!

Prayer:

Father God,

I know that I can do nothing without You. Because I believe in You, all things are possible for me. I submit my body to You so I can represent you well in the earth. I owe everything I am and everything I've got to You. Thank you for sending Jesus to rescue me from the traps in this world. I vow to listen to and obey Your voice. You speak loud and clear in Your Word and through the precious Holy Spirit that is in me. The Blood of Jesus covers and protects me from all harm. I am truly blessed! In Jesus' Mighty Name, Amen.

Reflections:

What do you give God the Glory for in your life?

Memory Verse: Mark 16:15 – 18 And He said to them, Go into all the world and preach and publish openly the good news (the Gospel) to every creature [of the whole human race]. He who believes [who adheres to and trusts in and relies on the Gospel and Him Whom it sets forth] and is baptized will be saved [from the penalty of eternal death]; but he who does not believe [who does not adhere to and trust in and rely on the Gospel and Him Whom it sets forth] will be condemned. And these attesting signs will accompany those who believe: in My name they will drive out demons; they will speak in new languages; They will pick up serpents; and [even] if they drink anything deadly, it will not hurt them; they will lay their hands on the sick; and they will get well.

Thought for the Day: The Great Commission!

Wow! This scripture proves that the main reason Jesus came to the Earth was to redeem fallen mankind. He was about to leave the Earth and take His seat at the right hand of the Father in heaven and left this assignment with His disciples. He commissioned them or gave them the power and authority to represent Him on the Earth. Just as He went all over the region that He lived in representing God His Father, He wanted His disciples to do the same. He advocated and publicly announced who God was and how much He loved us. He was constantly teaching the disciples and those who had the desire to hear what He was saying about the goodness of God. He brought hope to the hopeless, delivered those who were bound by the darkness and agents of darkness in the world as well as healed the sick (physically, mentally, and emotionally).

Just as He taught His disciples of that day to do what He was doing,

He wants us to do the same today. He has commissioned us to spread the Good news of the Gospel wherever we go. He wants everyone to know that they can be saved from the wrath of the evil one and rescued by His Spirit. He wants them to know that His Spirit will dwell in them, if they believe and receive Him to do so. The presence of His Spirit brings protection, healing, and wholeness. We have been given authority to lay hands on the sick and promised their recovery. We are the people who are to walk by faith, not by our senses or sight. Loving us the way He does, He did not want to leave without reminding us of the most important reason for being sent to the Earth. That is to impact everyone and everything in the Earth that we come in contact with using the power and authority given to us by God the Father, in Jesus Christ the Son, through the Holy Spirit who dwells in Us!

Declaration and Confession:

I have been chosen by God to spread the Good News about Jesus Christ, the Messiah. I will declare the goodness of God that was shown in Jesus Christ by the power of the Holy Spirit who lives in me! The assignment has been given, so I accept it and will deliver salvation, healing, and wholeness to a dying world!

Prayer:

Dear Lord Jesus,

Use me as an instrument of Your service. I confess my sins and You are faithful and just to cleanse me of all unrighteousness. Therefore, I am acceptable in Your sight to go forth with the might and power you have given me to bring healing and wholeness to those who are sick. I am an agent of light that will dispel the darkness in this Earth. Thank you for the privilege to serve You while I'm here in this Earth! In Jesus' Mighty Name, Amen.

Reflections:

When was the last time you allowed the Spirit of God to use you to spread the Good News of Jesus Christ?

Memory Verse: Colossians 3:18 – 21 Wives, be subject to your husbands [subordinate and adapt yourselves to them], as is right and fitting and your proper duty in the Lord. Husbands, love your wives [be affectionate and sympathetic with them] and do not be harsh or bitter or resentful toward them. Children, obey your parents in everything, for this is pleasing to the Lord. Fathers, do not provoke or irritate or fret your children [do not be hard on them or harass them], lest they become discouraged and sullen and morose and feel inferior and frustrated. [Do not break their spirit].

Thought for the Day: God's Modern Family

Although we have a different definition for the "family," God's meaning of what constitutes a family remains the same. He still intends for the family to have a father, mother, and children. The hierarchy He set up for the family still lists the husband/father (a male), as the head of the household. The wife/mother (a female) is second in command and subject to the desires of the husband. The children (whether male or female) are to be obedient to their parents (father and mother). When you look at His plan, it's very simplistic. We are the ones that make things complicated. We have twisted things into a pretzel, because we refuse to adhere to the ways God has ordained for us to respond. It's because of our disobedience that things are all messed up and the enemy is having a field day with the foundational system of our society. Without this system in place and operating the way it was ordained to function, we will remain in utter chaos!

The fact is we have more households without a father than ever before and the number is on the rise. We have adjusted God's plan to accommodate this abnormal pattern. It's so prevalent that we have accepted it as the norm. Just because some men have decided that they don't want to take on the responsibility of being a husband and/or father doesn't mean God has changed His mind. He still wants them to stand up and be counted as the trustworthy leaders of their family. The fact that they have abused their position as a husband or father leaving their families in shambles; doesn't dismiss God's desire for the family. Although we must commend those moms who have struggled and raised their children without a spouse and some men have done the same, this doesn't mean that this is God's best for the family. There are women who choose to take flight rather than using their motherly instincts to nurture a family. Some moms forfeit their child's relationship with a willing father to punish him for her own selfish reasons. Parents of both genders hold their children hostage to manipulate the other parent for a ransom. Children are disrespectful and spoiled. Many of them are physically, mentally, and emotionally abused by one or both of their parents who have done more than break their spirit. Yet, God's way demands that they obey their parents. Things are really a mess, but God hasn't changed His mind. The design for the family remains the same. The only way out of this mess is to read this scripture and follow its simple instructions. Is it too late? It's never too late to obey, repent and ask God to forgive us. All things are possible to them that Believe. The old family standards God set in motion from the beginning of time are still the standards God wants for His Modern Family!

Declaration and Confession:

I choose to be the kind of parent God has ordained that I be. I repent from any wrong I have done in the past or vow to operate God's way in the future. God is the same yesterday, today, and forever. He wants my family to be whole in every way. As a husband, I will love my wife and children the way God has ordained for me to love them. As a wife, I submit to the leadership of my husband. As a child, I will obey my parents. As a family, we will love one another unconditionally, as we are loved by God.

Prayer:

Father God,

Please forgive us for destroying the pattern You set in motion for the family. We repent for causing our families to be dysfunctional in so many ways. Holy Spirit we desperately need your help in changing the way we operate as fathers, mothers, and children. Teach us how to honor one another in our respective roles. Help us to keep God first and in the center of our relationships with one another. We ask all this in the mighty name of Jesus, Amen.

Reflections:

Whatever your family's current structure is, you can commit your family into the hands of our loving Father. Ask Him to give you the plan that He has for your family!

Memory Verse: Mark 11:13, 14, 20 And seeing in the distance a fig tree [covered] with leaves, He went to see if He could find any [fruit] on it [for in the fig tree the fruit appears at the same time as the leaves]. But when He came up to it, He found nothing but leaves, for the fig season had not yet come. And He said to it, No one ever again shall eat fruit from you. And His disciples were listening [to what He said]. In the morning, when they were passing along, they noticed that the fig tree was withered [completely] away to its roots.

Thought for the Day: Fruitless Reality!

---

*B*etween verse 14 to 20, Jesus travels on to Jerusalem with the disciples. When they get to the temple, He finds people selling and buying sacrifices in the porches and courts. The righteous indignation of God rose up in Him and He turned over the tables of the money changers and the seats of those dealing in the sale of doves. He also stopped the people from using the temple enclosure as a short-cut for travel. Why in the world was Jesus getting so upset? First of all, those selling the doves for sacrifice were taking advantage of the people by making a profit from a Godly requirement and selling inferior sacraments. In other words, there were certain requirements that needed to be followed in presenting your sacrifices to God. These requirements were not necessarily being followed and you know how people take advantage of those who have a pure heart towards God and look to those in charge to do what's right. They were unknowingly being led into a violation of the temple requirements! Also, greed has a way of creeping into the affairs of man. Another point to consider is what is involved in the presenting of a sacrifice for the person presenting it. It's more than just meeting an obligation. We found that out with Cain and Abel. God wants true repentance and real sacrifice of our substance and heart. He's not interested in the fast food mentality when it comes to obeying spiritual ordinances. The major problem was the attitude of disrespect the people had for the temple and the hard hearts of the chief priests and scribes who were in charge of running the temples. They were really ticked off with His interference of their management rules and income flow. Who does He think He is to come in and disturb their order of things? So, they continued to look for a way to get rid of Him, before His teachings totally turned the hearts of the people against them. They were called to represent the Kingdom of God, but their actions displayed fruitless production.

So it is with each of us. We have an obligation, as part of the Kingdom of God, to be what we are called to be. Whatever our life's purpose and assignment is, we need to be busy completing that! The fig tree was a fig tree in name only. It had beautiful green leaves, but there were no figs to harvest. It was not doing the job it was created to do. So, Jesus cursed it after He inspected it, because it was taking up space and time. Yet, it was producing Nothing! The Holy Spirit on the inside of us gives us the ability to produce the fruit of the Spirit. When we fail to produce love, joy, peace, patience, kindness, goodness, faithfulness, gentleness, and temperance; we are wonderfully and beautifully made while producing Nothing. Amongst our leaves, there must be fruit present in order for it to grow and mature. God gives us opportunities to get it together, but eventually there will come a time for our fruit to be inspected. If we are guilty of having fruitless production, we enter the possibility of living a cursed existence. The root is the unseen portion of our reality. What is the condition of our spirit or heart? God loves us and sent Jesus here so we could produce by the power of the Holy Spirit; He is a productive God! The reality of the situation is we don't want to be caught being FRUITLESS!

Declaration and Confession:

I want to be a Christian in word and in deed! I will produce love, joy, peace, patience, kindness, goodness, faithfulness, gentleness, and temperance! The Spirit of God in me will do the work in order for me to produce and be what God has called me to be. I will not be like that fig tree, living a cursed existence!

Prayer:

Dear Lord Jesus,

Help me to be what God has called me to be. Holy Spirit I surrender to you to do the work in me that is required for me to produce the fruit Jesus will inspect at the end of my existence. In Jesus' Mighty Name, Amen.

Reflections:

Are you a fruitless branch on the vine? Hopefully, you bear much fruit of the Spirit.

Memory Verse: John 5:30 - 32 I am able to do nothing from Myself [independently, of My own accord — but only as I am taught by God and as I get His orders]. Even as I hear, I judge [I decide as I am bidden to decide. As the voice comes to Me, so I give a decision], and My judgment is right (just, righteous), because I do not seek or consult My own will [I have no desire to do what is pleasing to Myself, My own aim, My own purpose] but only the will and pleasure of the Father Who sent me. If I alone testify in My behalf, My testimony is not valid and cannot be worth anything. There is Another Who testifies concerning Me, and I know and am certain that His evidence on My behalf is true and valid.

Thought for the Day: God Is My Witness!

When you are accused of wrong, the first thing the individual in charge does is ask for an eyewitness or witnesses to the wrong done. Just as those making the accusation must have proof of their accusation, so must the one being accused. Hopefully, someone can give you an alibi that clears you of the accusation being made. Either you were not even present to be guilty of the accusation or you have a legitimate defense for what you are being accused of. Many people have been convicted and sentenced for a wrong they were not guilty of because they could not produce evidence or a witness that could exonerate them from what they were accused of.

In this passage of scripture, Jesus is being accused of two things. One, He had just healed the impotent man at the Pool of Bethesda on the Sabbath and secondly, He was saying that He was the Son of God! The Jews were very angry about these two violations. After the man was healed, they questioned him about breaking the law that prohibited him from picking up his bed and walking on the Sabbath. They didn't seem to care about the welfare of the man at all. They were more concerned about their religious laws being broken. He explained that he was told by a man to pick up his bed. When they asked him who the man was, he could not tell them, because he did not know. Jesus located him later, pointed out the fact that he was healed, and told him not to sin anymore or something worse could happen to him. The man went to the Jews and told them it was Jesus who was responsible for his healing. The Jews were determined to kill Jesus for these violations. Jesus tried to explain the order of divine business He was operating in, but they did not have the spiritual ears necessary to hear what He was saying. They continued persecuting Him and seeking ways to kill Him instead. When we operate the way Jesus did in the Bible, we have the same problem. It is true that we can do nothing without the power and authority that comes from God and His Word. He vested that same power in Jesus and Jesus decided to pass that baton to us. But we have to accept Jesus as our Savior and Lord in order to hear what He is telling us to do. Then, after He tells us what to do, we have to be bold enough to stand against the wiles of the enemy and his cohorts to do what we're told. Once we have followed our divine instructions, all we can say is what Jesus said: "God is My Witness!"

Declaration and Confession:

I am determined to follow in the footsteps of Jesus! I know that His way of doing things is not the popular route to take in life. However, I get my directions from the divine Source of God! Jesus gets directions from His Heavenly Father and I do the same. We operate in harmony with God, Our Father!

Prayer:

Dear Lord Jesus,

I am depending on you for everything I do. I know I cannot make it without you on my side. I trust you to lead me in the direction I should go. When my actions are questioned, I point to Your Word to verify what I am doing. It's in the Name of Jesus that I do what I do. Father God is my witness! In Jesus' Mighty Name, Amen.

Reflections:

If you were put on trial today for your involvement in the Kingdom of God, would God be able to testify and convince the jury of your definite, divine involvement? Would you be guilty or innocent?

Memory Verse: Ephesians 3:19 – 21 [That you may really come] to know [practically, through experience for yourselves] the love of Christ, which far surpasses mere knowledge [without experience]; that you may be filled [through all your being] unto all the fullness of God [may have the richest measure of the divine Presence and become a body wholly filled and flooded with God Himself]! Now to Him Who, by (in consequence of) the [action of His] power that is at work within us, is able to [carry out His purpose and] do super-abundantly, far over and above all that we [dare] ask or think [infinitely beyond our highest prayers, desires, thoughts, hopes, or dreams] — To Him be glory in the church and in Christ Jesus throughout all generations forever and ever. Amen (so be it).

Thought for the Day: All Sufficient One!

This scripture far exceeds my ability to comprehend it! It's talking about a God who is El Shaddai, the ALL SUFFICIENT ONE! The only ONE capable of being everything that we need! This magnificent God is willing to live in us! He wants to worship with us and use us as a sanctuary for Him! We are allowed to be portable temples for Him! We are a living tabernacle for Him that represents refuge and protection from the evil of the day. Yet, we get to experience the same refuge and protection that we bring in us. How awesome is that! Without God, we can do or be nothing. With Him, we can do ALL Things through Christ who strengthens us to do and be! We can literally experience complete flooding by the Spirit of God who is in us! He will fill us to the point of overflow with Himself.

The purpose for our lives on this earth can only be obtained and carried out through the power of God that works in us to get the job done. He has to reveal our purpose to us and then, operate through us to complete the task at hand. All we have to do is submit to the mission that we have been assigned to. It is an impossible mission that is completely possible because of the God who is All Sufficient in us! I can hear the Mission Impossible theme music playing in my head right now! Our prayers, desires, thoughts, hopes, or dreams cannot come up with the master plan God has for each one of us to do. It is ALL God ordained and God completed. He gets ALL the Glory, Honor, and Praise for what He has done, is doing, and will do from generation to generation. This is too marvelous for our eyes of understanding! He is the ALL SUFFICIENT GOD!!!

Declaration and Confession:

I submit to the All Sufficient One, God the Father! I am nothing and can do nothing without Him! He provides every one of my needs and allows me to participate in His magnificent plan. I humbly submit to Him to do what He wills in and through me. I want Him to flood me with the power of His Holy Spirit. I want His presence to be evident in me. I want Him to use me as an instrument of His service to complete the mission that is impossible in the earth.

Prayer:

Father God,

Thank you for being my provider and protector! Without you, I can do nothing. Because of You, I am capable and able to do All things! I am covered by the precious Blood of Jesus and empowered by the Spirit of the Living God. I will get the job done that has been assigned to me and will be able to hear the voice of my Father say, "Well done my good and faithful servant! Come on up and receive your just reward." I believe and receive what El Shaddai has to give to me! In Jesus' Mighty Name, Amen.

Reflections:

God's grace is sufficient for you, because He is the All Sufficient One. You have unmerited favor, ask for what you want!

Memory Verse: John 10:14, 15, 27 I am the Good Shepherd; and I know and recognize My own, and My own know and recognize Me— Even as [truly as] the Father knows Me and I also know the Father—and I am giving My [very own] life and laying it down on behalf of the sheep. The sheep that are My own hear and are listening to My voice, and I know them, and they follow Me.

Thought for the Day: You Can Hear God!

Have you ever been in a crowded room full of children and parents? There could be hundreds of people present, but when your child cries out - "Mom!" or "Dad!" - your ears know that it's your child trying to get your attention. You gave birth to or fathered that child and you have developed a relationship with him or her from the beginning of their existence on this earth. The reason you know your child's voice is the same reason God knows your voice. He created you and knows all about you, even the number of hairs on your head. Surely he knows your voice or your cry! Even if the room is full of infants, you know the cry of your baby over all the others. Likewise, if all of us talk or cry at the same time, God still knows one voice from the other.

Normally, your child would also know your voice, because they have a relationship with you. You have been bonding and conversing with one another, so you know one another's voice. Unfortunately, many Christians I talk to tell me they don't hear the voice of their Heavenly Father. They say, "God doesn't talk to me." So I take them to these verses to show them that God listens, hears, and responds to their voice. Also, the Word says, they hear the voice of the Father, as well. We develop every relationship we have by talking to one another. We listen and respond.

Could it be that we talk, but we don't listen for the response from our Father? You would soon give up on a relationship with anyone who did all the talking and never gave you a chance to respond! I know that God talks back to us because the verse says the sheep hear, listen, and follow. If the Father didn't speak, we wouldn't know how to follow Him. However, the key here is, we have to listen to hear. We have to get quiet enough on the inside of ourselves to hear. Once our spiritual ears know the voice of God, we will hear Him above all others. We could be in a crowded room full of noise and still hear His voice. Why? Because we have trained ourselves to listen to His voice, so we can follow Him. If you haven't already, decide to put this scripture to work. YOU the sheep of the Good Shepherd, Can Hear the Voice of God!

Declaration and Confession:

I am a sheep of the Good Shepherd. I listen for and hear His voice, so I can follow His instructions for my life. I will not listen to the voice of the enemy. I will not allow what the world is saying to drown out the voice of My God! Once I hear His instructions, I will follow them!

Prayer:

Dear Lord Jesus,

You are the Good Shepherd who watches over His sheep. Thank you for loving me enough to give your life for me. My ears are attentive to your voice. You lead me in the path of righteousness for your name sake. You hear my cry and come to my rescue. Thank you for protecting me. I am your sheep and I hear your voice, daily. In Jesus' Mighty Name, Amen.

Reflections:

Are you familiar with your Father's voice? If not, He's waiting to have a two-way conversation with you!

Memory Verse: Proverbs 3:5 – 8 Lean on, trust in, and be confident in the Lord with all your heart and mind and do not rely on your own insight or understanding. In all your ways know, recognize, and acknowledge Him, and He will direct and make straight and plain your paths. Be not wise in your own eyes; reverently fear and worship the Lord and turn [entirely] away from evil. It shall be health to your nerves and sinews, and marrow and moistening to your bones.

Thought of the Day: Trust God Daily!

---

*H*ave you ever heard someone say, "I'm a nervous wreck?" That's what you become, when you're trying to run your life according to your understanding of things. There's so much we don't know or understand that when we try to manage our own lives, we will totally mess up! We really don't want to become dry, unhealthy bones. So our best bet is to consult the God of the universe. He knows the beginning, middle, and end happenings of our life. It's like having the answer key to a test you are about to take. If we understood that simple analogy, we would ace the test of life every time!

Most of us work really hard at trying to live life doing and being right. The problem is that hindsight is 20/20, but current sight is cloudy. We just don't see things the way they truly are. There are times that the enemy blocks our view, so we just don't see things clearly. Sometimes our own judgment is out of focus and at other times we allow someone who doesn't navigate their own life properly to give us directions. Most times, we simply don't have all of the details in a given situation. But our Father does! All we really have to do is lean, trust, and be confident in God, who is the author and finisher of our faith. Our life's story has already been written by Him. If we recognize and acknowledge His significance in our life from the beginning, we will start off on the right path. We must be careful not to yield to our limited view of things and start making decisions based on how we think or feel. The wisdom of God is needed daily to stay on the right path. A detour could cost us years of rescue and reconstruction. So continuous acknowledgement and trust is needed throughout our journey because we want the middle of our lives to be just as strong or even stronger than the beginning. As we gain wisdom and continue to fear the awesome God we serve, worship will be part of our daily lifestyle. We will realize that we just cannot worship and praise Him enough! The Spirit of God in us will sharpen our sight and we will stay focused on Jesus. As long as we keep our eyes on Him, we will not succumb to the evil around us. We will miss the pitfalls that are put in our way and navigate around the obstacles put in our path. All the way to the end of our lives, we'll have clarity in the direction and purpose for our life. The summary of our life will include calm nerves, spiritual muscles and strength that bring nourishment through the Word of God that replenishes our soul. Even our bones will be restored through the washing of the water of God's Word. We MUST Trust God Daily!

Declaration and Confession:

I am confident in the God of my salvation! I can lean on and trust Him with my life! His wisdom and understanding surpasses mine. With my whole heart and mind I rely on His insight and understanding. He directs my path as I recognize and acknowledge Him. I fear and worship Him. I want to live a life that is void of evil. I Trust Him Daily!

Prayer:

Father God,

I trust you with my whole heart! I have learned to lean and depend on you. Your insight and understanding take away the guessing that I do when I try to direct myself. I worship and adore You for who You are in my life! You bring health to my nerves, sinews, marrow and moisten my bones. I honor You with all that I am! Help me to steer clear of evil. I Trust You Daily. In Jesus' Mighty Name, Amen.

Reflections:

Based on this devotional entry, what are you trusting God for today?